PUBLISHED BY BAISDEN PUBLISHING LLC

Other Books
by Michael Baisden

Maintenance Man II

Do Men Know What They Want?

God's Gift To Women

The Maintenance Man

Men Cry In The Dark

Never Satisfied

■ ■ ■

Do Women Know What They Want? (DVD)

Love, Lust & Lies (DVD)

Do Women Know What They Want?
Reunion TV Special (DVD)

RAISE YOUR HAND IF YOU HAVE ISSUES

IF YOU DIDN'T RAISE YOUR HAND YOU'RE **LYING** AND THAT'S AN **ISSUE**

MICHAEL BAISDEN

PUBLISHED BY BAISDEN PUBLISHING LLC
Copyright © 2013 All Rights Reserved.

LEARN MORE BY VISITING WWW.BAISDENLIVE.COM
Like Michael on Facebook at BaisdenLive
Follow Michael on Twitter @BaisdenLive

Published By: Baisden Publishing LLC
www.BaisdenLive.com

Stories used in this book are based on interviews, were penned anonymously, are public domain or were written by Michael Baisden.

Cover Design by Charles Allan Smith / George Achi - Earthbeat Productions
N Squared Design Studio

Book Design by Stacy Luecker - Essex Graphix

Cover Photo by Charles Allan Smith - Earthbeat Productions

Printed in the United States of America
First Printing

ISBN-10: 0984776583
ISBN-13: 978-0-9847765-8-0

Dedication

To all the people who have issues ... like me!

~ Michael Baisden

Table of Contents

RAISE YOUR HAND IF YOU HAVE ISSUES

IF YOU DIDN'T RAISE YOUR HAND YOU'RE **LYING** AND THAT'S AN **ISSUE**

Introduction

As I sit here typing the first lines of this book, a cool breeze is blowing through my balcony window. I'm looking out on the ocean and wondering whether this book will impact the lives of those who read it. I mean, what's the point of writing if the goal isn't to inspire people to look deeper into themselves? Or at the very least challenge them to see things from a different perspective?

For the past 20 years I've written five best-selling books, spoken at standing-room-only seminars, hosted two television shows, had two of my novels adapted to stage plays, and hosted a national radio show reaching 7 million people in over 100 cities. But none of those things would have happened if I didn't deal with my issues of fear. I was afraid to walk away from my job; afraid I wouldn't be able to provide for my daughter; afraid of failure. Those are some pretty big issues, especially for a college dropout whose only job experience was four years in the U.S. Air Force.

But after self-publishing my first book, *Never Satisfied*, back in January 1995 and selling 50,000 copies at events and out of the trunk of my car, I gained the confidence I needed to walk away from my job as a train conductor for the Chicago Transit Authority (CTA), and I haven't looked back.

In hindsight I realized that my success not only came from dealing with my own issues of fear, doubt and other insecurities, but also mastering my reaction to other people's issues. Those people who try to discourage you and block your dreams, *they* have issues! The trick is not to make their issues your issues, but instead use them to motivate you. Once I made up my mind to be a writer, I avoided everything and everybody not supportive of that dream. Or as I like to call them, "Dream Thieves!"

The inspiration for this book came from interaction with my Facebook Friends. I call them my "Dream Supporters, my Family." Three years ago I began greeting them each morning with an inspirational quote, and each night I would post my commentary on topics of love, self-esteem, family and success.

That casual practice became an obsession for my Facebook Friends and me. But it also challenged me to dig deeper each day to produce more thoughtful quotes or ideas, which, in turn, challenged them to respond. And that's when I discovered my purpose in life — to challenge people to think, and to encourage and engage them to think outside the box. It was that gift that took this college dropout and former CTA train conductor from the South Side of Chicago to leading thousands in civil rights marches, helping to elect the first Black President, and speaking to millions over the airwaves about domestic violence, molestation, infidelity, mentoring, health and, of course, living their dream.

I learned early in my career that being successful is not always about having all the answers; it's knowing how to ask the right questions and being willing to listen to perspectives that are different from your own. I would often tell my listeners, "If you're not willing to have an open mind to other points of view, you'll never grow!"

I have been blessed to have fans who don't simply agree with everything I say; they take my comments and use them to elevate the conversation. That's what we're missing in society today: quality, engaging, thought-provoking dialogue. I hope this book will help change that. God knows we can use some mental stimulation, especially with all the dumbing down on TV and radio, especially with our young people.

Some might ask what my credentials are to write this book. Well, I've been happily married and happily divorced; had my heart broken and broken a few hearts; made mistakes as a parent and graduated a child from college; and failed miserably at business and had tremendous success! You don't need a piece of paper to promote critical thinking and common sense; I have a PhD in this thing called life.

But the most important qualification of all is that I have issues, too.

Toxic People

Raise Your Hand
If You Have Issues

Of course I have issues, who doesn't? There are so many I can almost guarantee you there will be a part two to this book. I have issues with relationships, issues with bad parenting, issues with people who block other people's dreams, and I have plain old everyday issues, like people who drive too slow in the left lane on the highway. Doesn't that drive you crazy?

I have issues with men who cheat and the women who tolerate it. I have issues with deadbeat parents and parents who use their children as pawns for revenge. I have issues with women who lie about paternity and men who say they don't want to be a father but refuse to wear protection. I have issues with women who constantly say, "All the men I date are dogs!" but don't take responsibility for the fact that they are the ones choosing them!

I have issues with parents who leave their children in the care of strangers or relatives who abuse them, then when they are told about the abuse, they blame the innocent child. I hope some of you parents are listening because that's a serious issue.

I have issues with young people who wear their pants so low you can see their dirty underwear and adults who complain but never confront them about it. I have issues with people who complain about how bad the country is but don't vote on Election Day. My attitude is this: If you don't vote, you don't get to complain, so shut up!

I have issues with Dream Killers who do everything in their power to discourage, sabotage and laugh you out of pursuing your dream.

But I also have issues with those who allow the naysayers to win. Every successful person has a story about overcoming adversity. Use that negative energy as motivation to prove them wrong; better yet, just do it for yourself. Who cares what they think anyway?

I have issues with insecure men and jealous women who pray for the ideal mate but when they find him or her, they can't handle it. And speaking of prayer, I have issues with church folks who are quick to judge but don't have their own lives together.

But my biggest issue of them all is with people who don't think they have issues. According to them, they are never wrong! It's always someone else's fault, someone else's problem; everyone is wrong except them! If you are one of those people, this book was written especially for you. No matter how wrong the other person was for hurting you, either you participated, instigated or ignored the signs. In other words, it takes two to tango.

Hopefully this will help you snap out of your state of denial. As the slogan goes in Alcoholics Anonymous, "The first step to recovery is admission."

Now raise your hand if you have issues!

I'm Allergic
To Negative People

I have issues with negative people! And there are some days where it feels like every negative person in the universe was put in my path to aggravate me. But unlike most people I have the luxury of working from home. That's what's great about writing; it's a secluded occupation. But I remember the days of fighting rush-hour traffic on the Dan Ryan Expressway when I was growing up in Chicago, and that hellish bumper-to-bumper traffic on 405 in Los Angeles when I was shooting my TV show, "Talk or Walk." I was so stressed by the time I arrived at the studio, I needed a hot stone massage and a pot of coffee just to decompress. "How do people do this every day?" I would say to myself. The show was eventually canceled, which was a sad day. I missed my crew and the incredible show guests. But I didn't miss that damned traffic, let me tell you.

And driving back home was no better. You would think that people would be in a hurry to get home after work but the traffic would move even slower. Every day I would stress out running red lights rushing to get back to my quiet and serene apartment. Meanwhile, everyone was driving as if they were dreading making it home. My attitude is, if you're not rushing to get home, you're probably not in the right relationship.

Every day I make it my business to try to speak to everyone who crosses my path, at least the ones I make close eye contact with. Sometimes it can be a simple nod of the head; other times I'll just blurt out, "Hello!" It shocks the hell out of people, too, especially when you do it on an elevator. Most people try to avoid making eye contact or speaking to you. That's a challenge to me, so I'll wait until everyone is on and the doors close, and then I'll say, "Good morning!" real loud. Most of the time people are pleasant and will smile and respond back. But some people are grouchy no matter how polite you are. The sun could be shining bright on a beautiful spring day and they would have something negative to say.

But what are they so unhappy about? Americans need to take their lazy behinds over to some parts of Africa, Asia and the Caribbean so they can see what real poverty is. We can walk into a library seven days a week and read books all day in an air-conditioned room, with perfect lighting, fresh water and carpet on the floor. And if you get hungry there are at least two dozen restaurants within walking distance. In some parts of the world a book is a luxury, electricity is nonexistent, and the closest food may be several miles away. What the hell are we so negative about? We are by far the most ungrateful nation on the planet — and we have the most ungrateful children.

Kids today complain if their flat screen is not big enough, or if it doesn't have a feature for 3D. When we were growing up we were lucky to have one television in the entire house, and even then you only got three or four channels. Children nowadays have their own 40-inch flat screen, their own computer, their own room, and they can watch television around the clock. Back in the day, television use to go off! Y'all remember that? At about 2 o'clock in the morning, "The Star-Spangled Banner" would start playing and that was it, lights out! So what are kids so negative and unhappy about? They have it all! Children should be walking around with a smile surgically sculpted onto their little faces.

But being positive has nothing to do with possessions. If that were true most people would have a positive attitude. The reality is just the reverse; people have put so much value on "things" that they are bankrupt in every other aspect of their lives. We don't have as many close friends as we used to, and there's less time for family. Families used to eat together at the dinner table, and neighbors aren't neighborly like they used to be. Back in the day, we knew who lived in every house for a 10-block radius, and I'm not exaggerating. Now you're lucky if you even know the first and last names of the people who live next door. How bad has it gotten when you can't even start your day with a pleasant "Good morning!" from your neighbor? Now that's some fragernackle bull!

Carolyn is the perfect example of a woman who knows how to manage toxic people. As the only single woman in her subdivision she has to deal with jealousy and racism at the same time. But as I interviewed her for this story, it was obvious she had everything under control. She was determined not to allow their issues to become her issues.

Carolyn's Story: People Are A Trip!

People crack me up, they waste so much time and energy being hateful when they could use half that to be nice and cordial. First there's my racist next-door neighbor who intentionally rushes out of her garage five minutes before she knows that I do just so she doesn't have to acknowledge me. I just sit there in the kitchen watching out my window laughing as I sip on my cup of tea. She damn near knocked over her garbage can the other day she was so frantic to avoid greeting me. People can be so petty.

My job moved me to Orlando from Chicago six months ago and it's been a struggle making friends in my complex, and being the only black person and single doesn't help. All of the white and Hispanic husbands are so sweet to me, they rush over to help out when I have groceries or if I'm having problems with my lawn mower. The wives hate it! I'm single and living in a home just as expensive as the ones they live in, and for some people that's an issue. But what's really driving them crazy is that I look good! Most of the women in my subdivision are stay-at-home moms and many of them have let themselves go. Hey, that's not my fault. Even though I have a full-time job I still make time for the gym every day. Don't hate, emulate, I always say.

I make it my business not to start my day by taking calls from gossiping girlfriends and family members with issues. I believe that starting your day on a positive note is critical. Besides, most of the time people are not talking about anything different from day to day; it's a repeat of all the other drama they had the week before. Why should I waste my time listening to a problem you have no intention of correcting? And the few times I do listen, I'm usually multitasking. Half the time I'm focusing on something else while they're yapping. "Umm-hum, for real, is that right?" Meanwhile, I'm working on a report for work or doing sit-ups.

I'll be damned if I'm going to put my life on pause while they go on and on for hours about absolutely nothing! And as for watching bad news on TV, that's not an issue because I don't own a television set. Why should I pay for cable when I can watch every show I like on my computer, without all the commercials? I dislike hearing bad news in the morning, and that's all news is. They find the worst stories in the country and replay them over and over again. And if there's no bad news in the U.S. they will bring you a murder, suicide or bombing attack from overseas. What kind of way is that to start your day?

It has taken me 35 years to get some balance to my life and I accomplished that by limiting the number of people I give my number and e-mail to, and blocking anyone on my social network who is not in my circle. Having a peaceful life doesn't happen by accident. You have to design it and then train people how to interact with you. My friends already know I'm not the one to call in the morning with drama. And as for missing television, it keeps unwanted company from coming over and getting too comfortable. If you're not a reader this is not the destination for you. Besides, who needs TV? I couldn't stand it when the commercials were twice as loud as the TV program. That's reason enough to get rid of cable.

■ ■ ■

Carolyn's story is so similar to mine it's ridiculous. Maybe that's why I chose it. It's encouraging to hear someone who thinks like you do, someone who understands the importance of having peace of mind. I'm sure not everyone means to be negative but that's beside the point. It's all about protecting our mind from toxic influences, whether they are intended or not. The best way to help negative people is by refusing to co-sign on their unhealthy behavior; that's just enabling them. I've lost a lot of friends over the years because they were unable to move forward mentally, spiritually and in terms of being more positive and open-minded.

No matter how much you love your friends, family, and even your partner, sometimes people get stuck. I'm not saying stop loving them, but in order to continue your journey through life, you have to love them from a distance.

Every successful person has a story to tell about how they were discouraged, sabotaged and laughed at. But those things only make you more determined to prove the naysayers wrong.

Having people cheer you on is great, but there's something about getting pissed off that takes your motivation to another level.

~ Michael Baisden

Dream Killers

Throughout my career as a writer, speaker, TV personality and radio host, I've had to deal with people trying to block, sabotage and outright destroy my dreams. When "The Haters" begin to see you rise they will do anything to keep you from succeeding. I've had people lie, cheat, steal, forge signatures on contracts, spread rumors, and conspire in the hopes that I would either quit or do things their way. And that was happening with major corporations with CEOs and major players in the broadcasting industry. The higher you climb, the more powerful the resistance. It's important to understand this going into the game of business. When millions of dollars are at stake, morals and ethics often go right out the window. People you thought you could trust will stab you in the back in a minute for that almighty dollar.

Fortunately for me, I had a loyal staff and a great manager who watched my back; that helped to minimize the damage. That's another important lesson that should be taught in every business school: "Build your team if you want to realize your dream!" And that building process happens on a daily basis with everyone you come into contact with, from the FedEx and UPS drivers to the guy working at the car wash. Every interaction is a potential customer or contact. That's why integrity and character are so critical to long-term success — you never know who is going to help take your business to the next level. When you're serious about building your dream, everyone you meet falls into one of two categories: "Dream Supporters" or "Dream Killers." There are no neutral people in the life of an entrepreneur. Don't ever forget that!

When you step out on faith you'll need all the help you can get because chances are you are going to fall flat on your face more than a few times before you find your way. I'm not saying you need "Yes Men," but you will definitely need people around you who will pick you up when you fall and cheer you on. No matter how smart and ambitious you may think you are, failure is guaranteed and naysayers will be right there waiting to tell you, "See, I told you that idea wouldn't work!" Or, as in my case, "I told you nobody was going to pay for your book!" Dream Killers live for the moment where they can say, "I told you so!"

But failure is a necessary step to success. My story is no different; I went bankrupt and had a failed marriage on my way to success. I remember telling my then-wife, "Something is going on in my life and I need to remove myself from this situation if I want it to happen." She was an incredible wife, but the marriage was not healthy for either one of us. It was great that we were able to remain friends but my destiny was calling me, and it was speaking loudly. After we separated I moved into an apartment with nothing but a waterbed, kitchen table, TV set that I had on crates, cheap desk and my computer. That was the beginning of Legacy Publishing. I borrowed $1,000 from two of my fellow co-workers, Louis Salazar and Rodney Julian, and another thousand from my mother. That was the investment that allowed me to set out to live my dream of becoming a writer.

But while all of this was happening, there were people all around me doubting that I could do it. Even when my manuscript was done and everyone was complimenting me on writing a 300-page book, there were many others quietly hoping I would fail. Some of you have had this same experience. You get so tired of people being negative you just stop sharing your dream altogether, and that's a good idea. It's a mistake to share your dream with Dream Killers. The more you tell them, the more reason they give you for why it won't work. And the closer you get to your dream, the more hateful they become.

It's one thing to have your friends and co-workers blocking and sabotaging your dream, but when it comes from family and the person you love, it can be devastating. Yes, parents kill their kids' dreams. Cousins, aunts and uncles do, too. Even a husband or wife can put a dagger in your back if they believe your dream will take you away from them or, more accurately, grow you out of them. That's why for many authors, artists and business owners, stepping out on faith often means stepping out of your area code, your city, your state and possibly your country. Nearly every story I've heard from hugely successful people is that their careers only took off after they left their hometowns. My theory is that people you grow up with have a hard time accepting you as anything other than the kid who grew up next door, or that guy from the mailroom. I was a train conductor for eight years, and many of my co-workers just couldn't envision me as a national celebrity. And I don't think it was necessarily because of jealousy; some people simply find it impossible to see you outside of the person they are used to. Just because you have a vision for yourself doesn't mean everyone else shares it. It wasn't until years later when I had my own television show that people finally realized, "Michael is not coming back to work on the trains! He really did make it!"

I'll never forget the day I decided to leave my job at the Chicago Transit Authority. I awoke looking up at the ceiling, then I rolled off my bed onto the floor and started praying so hard that tears poured down my face. I knew it was time, I knew I was ready, and I knew that day I was going to make my move. That's a moment in the life of every entrepreneur that you never forget. I call it "The Moment of Truth." Do you believe in yourself or not? Well, I did! After wiping the tears from my face, I gathered up my equipment and walked into the living room and called my mother.

"Hey, Mom. I'm going to do it!" I told her. "I'm quitting my job at the CTA today!"

She didn't pause one second.

"Good for you, baby. I believe in you. You can do it!"

Although there was no doubt in my mind about leaving, it made me even more confident about my decision when she gave me her blessing. And that's the point of this story; I was building my team years before I wrote that book. I built relationships with the co-workers who believed in my dream enough to invest their money; my mother invested money and was cheering me on! Even my ex-wife helped out by cooking meals and proofreading my first book, *Never Satisfied*. They were my Dream Team! And while I'm giving credit where it's due, I must also give a special thanks to all my fellow Chicago Transit employees and passengers who acted as unofficial editors and proofreaders. Their constructive criticism and encouragement got me through a lot of tough days and writer's block. They were an important part of the team, too. Those were my dream supporters back in 1994, and I haven't looked back since!

So who's on your team? If you ever expect to escape that 9-to-5 *Shawshank Redemption* job you hate, you'd better start taking inventory of the people in your circle! Remember, there are no neutral people in the life of a serious business-man or businesswoman. Everyone must contribute, assist, support, network and bring something of value to the table. I was lucky, I had people around me who nurtured and supported my dream, but I also lost people along the way. People I thought were true friends. That is, until I started talking about leaving my job and having all these big ideas about being somebody! All of a sudden their energy shifted and the attacks began. One incident stands out in my mind to this very day. I was at a co-worker's apartment with my buddies watching a Chicago Bulls game. My friend invited some ladies over to join us. During halftime, or at some point when there was a timeout, I began talking to the ladies about my book and my plans to leave my job. They were completely immersed in the conversation and supportive of my plans to be a full-time writer. Suddenly, my friends jumped in telling jokes and laughing, saying, "You don't know how to write a book! And besides, who in the hell is going to publish a book by an unknown author?"

I calmly got up, said goodbye, and walked out the door. As I got into my car and drove off, I was fuming. I knew then that I would never see those guys again. Maybe as co-workers, but not as friends. And I kept my word. One of the guys who was there came around some months later, and we remained close friends until the radio job happened in New York in 2003. But that friendship ended when I pressed him to do more with his life. I saw him getting comfortable with his success and I was nowhere near where I wanted to be, and I'm still not. So we went our separate ways and that was the close of that chapter. Some years later he showed up at an Expo in Chicago and just walked up to me and said, "I just came here to tell you, you were right! I *was* getting too comfortable." He gave me his business card and walked away. That's the last time I saw or heard from him.

I'm telling you this story because if you are determined to live your dream you will have similar stories. Not everyone is meant to go on this journey with you. Have you heard the expression "For a season, for a reason, and for a lifetime"? Well, that's true! Don't feel guilty if you have to move on without the people you started with. Understand that sometimes friends, acquaintances, employees, managers and even spouses serve a specific purpose at that specific time in your life. I know that may sound cold but that's the way it is. Sometimes the test itself is to see whether or not you have the strength to let go.

When we don't have the confidence or conviction to move on because we're too concerned about hurting someone's feelings, then we become our own Dream Killers!

There is no such thing as a neutral relationship. Our friendships and marriages either move us forward or hold us back!

Starting today, evaluate what kind of relationships you're in and then ask yourself, "Is this person moving me closer to fulfilling my dreams or farther away?"

~ Michael Baisden

Sleeping With The Enemy

There are few things that will strain a relationship more than starting a business. Some people naively go into business believing they can easily balance home life and business life, but that's easier said than done. Getting a business off the ground is one of the most stressful and demanding experiences you'll ever have. During those critical first three to five years, there's no such thing as balance. And that is why you often hear people refer to their business as "My Baby" — because they have to nurture it 24/7 in order for it to survive. In fact, I think it requires just as much time and energy as a real child, if not more! And the person who needs to understand that more than anyone else is the significant other who will be asked to take a back seat to his or her partner's dream. For some spouses it's a welcome challenge; for others, it may as well be a summons to divorce court.

There are two different types of what I call "Intimate Business Relationships." One is where the business existed before the couple entered into the relationship, and the other is where the business is created after they become involved or after marriage. There are challenges in both situations, but even more so if neither partner has been a business owner. That's when the odds increase for the creation of a "Dream Killer."

If one of the partners has been an entrepreneur, he or she will understand the demands it brings, such as out-of-town meetings, calls at all hours of the night, last-minute schedule changes with family and, most importantly, constant networking. That means talking to strangers and passing out business cards nearly everywhere you go. Entrepreneurs are rarely, if ever, off the clock. If your spouse is secure and sees your dream as being something that will benefit the family, they'll be right beside you, hustling and pitching. But if they become insecure and jealous and begin to see every attractive person you talk to as a threat, watch out, things will began to quickly unravel!

But let me be clear, you have a responsibility to not contribute to your partner's insecurity. Too often entrepreneurs become consumed with making money and getting the next deal signed to the point of forgetting that there's someone waiting at home who was responsible, in part, for them being successful in the first place. And even if your partner is only playing a supportive role, they always want to be made to feel like a priority in your life, not *the* priority, but a priority. Although it may be difficult to keep a balance as a business owner, you should always try to make your partner feel special. If you can't do that, then you shouldn't be in a relationship in the first place.

■ ■ ■

Since this chapter also deals with Dream Killers, let's assume the entrepreneur is conducting himself or herself with professionalism and with respect towards their partner. The objective now is to grow the business and, ideally, to grow the relationship simultaneously. In fact, building a company can test your patience, intelligence, creativity and resourcefulness like nothing else; it builds character, and that can be a positive thing for a relationship.

But what self-employment also does is expose the weakness in your marriage. Ask any couple who has built a strong business together and they will tell you that success is a team sport. When you walk into a room with your significant other, you are being judged by their presentation as much as your own. I've seen million-dollar deals quickly go south because the spouse made a bad impression. Your partner should be your best foot forward, not the weakest link!

So which one best describes your partner? If you don't know the answer to that question, being in a business setting for just a short period of time will answer it for you.

Theresa is the best example of both "Intimate Business Relationship" situations. When she met her husband she was running a successful temp agency. Two years after they married, she sold her businesses to become a stay-at-home mom. But after her son was old enough to go to kindergarten she was ready to start hustling again.

Theresa's Story: Issues Of Trust

"Once an entrepreneur, always an entrepreneur." Those are the exact words I told my husband when I shut down my temp agency to be a stay-at-home mom and housewife. I made it crystal clear that as soon as Jaylan was old enough for kindergarten I was going back into business. I sold my previous businesses for a nice profit so money wasn't an issue. And I made sure to check in every week or two to remind him of my plans. Sometimes men can come down with a case of selective amnesia so I made sure to keep things in the front of his mind. I love taking care of my family, but I was determined not to become Suzie Homemaker for the rest of my life.

In August, two months after Jaylan turned 5, I was the first one in line to sign up for the fall kindergarten. I did my research, got references from several parents and read the reviews online. A week later I dropped him off and went back to hustling. It felt good, too! I missed having meetings and networking with all kinds of people. I traveled all over the world with the temp agency. I had satellite offices in Indonesia, India and Mexico. If you ever called customer service for one of the major cell phone companies, you were probably talking to one of my people.

And those contacts paid off when I decided to go in another direction and open a concierge service. I had a Rolodex of celebrities and CEOs, many of whom were sponsors or pitch people for the companies I previously had contracts with. Most people don't understand that being successful in business is all about relationships. And before I knew it, the clients and money were rolling in.

To keep my life simple, I only worked with clients who were older and more established. I didn't have time for the nonsense some of these young athletes and artists take you through. I only made one exception; I did a little talent management on the side with an up-and-coming young actor, which would come back to bite me in the butt later. But for the moment, my husband loved it! I got tickets to the Lakers games, backstage passes to concerts, we even went on a couple of sets of major movie productions. You name it, we were there, and in the VIP section!

But all that came to an end one day when we were at a red carpet party for the young actor I mentioned earlier. I'll call him Damien. It didn't help that leading up to that event he had been staying out much later than usual working with a contractor to get his new house in order before he moved from New York. While I was sitting at the bar, Damien walked over to me, grabbed me by the waist and gave me a big hug and a peck on the cheek. "Thanks for everything, Reesie!" Then he smiled and walked away. My husband, who was returning from the restroom, saw the whole thing. Even though it was completely innocent, he went off! Not right away; he gave me the silent treatment for the rest of the evening and waited until we got to the car, then he let me have it!

"What the hell was that all about?"

"Honey, this is Hollywood, that's how we greet each other."

"Well, I'm from Louisiana, and where I'm from that's inappropriate."

"Baby, look, there is nothing going on between me and my clients. I conduct myself like a professional, and that's why I get paid like a professional. I'm good at what I do!"

"Maybe a little too good!"

"What in the hell is that supposed to mean?"

"You figure it out!"

Again, I got the silent treatment. Not just for the ride home but for the next two days. After he calmed down he insisted that I resign from working with Damien. But I explained to him that once the word got out that I quit a client, my business was over, and with no explanation except that I have an insecure husband.

The part that pissed me off most was that he was fine as

long as my job served the purpose of going to basketball games and getting concert tickets and autographs, but the minute he felt threatened by a rich, young, attractive man, all bets were off. I love my husband and I'm not going anywhere. But men seem to have a problem when their woman is in control of her own life and making her own money, and God forbid she's making more money than he is, which is the case with me. I'm already out-earning my husband two to one. But instead of seeing the benefits of their woman's success, they start trippin'. And most often because they think that we think like they do. Just because they would screw somebody they think we will, too. Men can be so shallow!

The bottom line for any woman who is trying to balance a relationship and a business is this: Always respect your man and reassure him as much as possible, but never, and I mean never, allow his issues to stop you from making your own money. If you know you're being faithful, challenge him to accept it, or he can go kick rocks. And that's coming from a woman who loves her man to death. But if he really loves you he'll never give you an ultimatum to choose between him and your dream.

■ ■ ■

Theresa's point goes both ways; a woman should never give her man an ultimatum or block his dreams, either. A man defines himself by what he does for a living. His business in many ways is his identity. A woman can be the best CEO in the world but in this sexist society she often gets more credit for raising great kids and being a good wife. It's not like that for a man; we are what we do, period! And it's also the way many women judge us, if they're honest enough to admit it. And for a man who is serious about his business, it's about much more than making money and having the title of President on a business card. His business is his freedom from "The Man!" Not just economic freedom but creative freedom.

If he has an idea in the shower that morning, he can make it happen that afternoon, and he doesn't have to run it up the corporate ladder for approval. For most business owners that's what it's all about — freedom! A quote I read many years ago says it all. It read, "A person will never be truly happy until they are engaged in something creative."

Most entrepreneurs are artists, in the sense that we must think creatively every day to adapt to our environment, write a new book, produce a new song or figure out a way to save money. Those things require creativity. So when a man's wife or girlfriend tries to kill his dream, she is not only threatening to kill his income, she's killing his outlet for creativity. A true entrepreneur will fight until the death to protect that! He will not allow her to sabotage his dream and send him back to corporate America where he is unappreciated and emasculated.

And who better to understand the sacrifice and importance of creativity than another businessperson or artist? The biggest threats to an unhappy relationship are the people your man comes in contact with every day — his customers, his clients, his business partners and his fans. It doesn't take a rocket scientist to figure out that if a man is not being supported at home, that woman who is stroking his ego every day and cheering him on is more likely to become his next partner.

Of course, none of that would matter if his relationship at home was solid, but just as men can become very insecure, so can women. As his business begins to take off, the wife or girlfriend notices a change in her man. The person she saw dragging in exhausted late at night with dirt under his nails or in his sweaty uniform is now working out at the gym, wearing nice suits and attending power lunches downtown. He's got swagger!

He barely resembles the man she married a few years back, but in his mind he's the man he always knew he could be; all he needs now is someone who believes in him to get to the next level. Of course, that person should be the wife or girlfriend, but she's so busy worrying about losing him that she's missing her opportunity to step up and be a true partner. It's not that she doesn't love him or doesn't want to see him succeed. The problem is she doesn't feel worthy of this new man. He's outgrown her and she knows it. Somewhere deep down inside she doesn't see herself in his future, and over time her low self-esteem becomes apparent to him and he also loses the vision of them being together in his next chapter.

He didn't want it that way, but she left him no choice. Her insecurity forces him to make a choice between a relationship that was going nowhere and a dream that can take him places he never imagined. It's no competition for the entrepreneur with a vision. The dream always wins out. If your partner can't stay in the boat while it's rocking, maybe they weren't supposed to be in your boat. Just saying.

■ ■ ■

I was determined to end this chapter on a positive note instead of the final word being about the "Dream Killers." I wanted to highlight the dream supporters. While I was writing this book, I posted on the topic of "Sleeping with the enemy" and received a very inspirational letter from a woman named Harriet. This is her story.

Harriet's Story: Stand By Your Man

When my husband graduated from MSU, they had just instituted the National Teachers Exam. When we took it, no one told us that we had to make a 950. We just knew we had to take it. When the scores came out, that's when we found out that there was a cutoff. He missed it by one point — 949! That meant he could not teach.

After four years, he had a piece of paper that meant nothing! So he spent the first year after receiving a degree doing the only job he could find. He worked with the school maintenance department cutting grass and repairing whatever needed to be done. I was a teacher at the school where he had to mow. When I would see him, I'd go out to wave and talk for a minute. My students couldn't believe that my husband was the maintenance man. As a former college basketball star, it was difficult to go from the roar of the crowd to the roar of the mower.

Students and friends laughed at him but it never broke him. It only made him more determined to succeed. For the next year, he studied every night. I mean, EVERY night. No matter what, he picked up that study guide. On his next try, he passed the test. He went on to be a teacher/coach and high school principal, he attended the Harvard Institute for Principals, became Principal of the Year, and retired after over 25 years as an educator. He overcame the negative situation and the negative people!

■ ■ ■

I admired Harriet's husband for his perseverance. I wrote her back and told her to let her husband know he was my hero. As a man who has been out of work and disrespected by friends and associates, I empathize with his struggle and celebrate his success! Bravo, Principal.

You know it's easy to label people as Dream Killers, but let me offer you a different perspective. When people respond negatively about your goals and dreams, it's not always because they don't want to see you succeed. Sometimes they know you are that special one who has the talent and passion to be great and they don't want you to leave and take that "light" with you.

I know I was the one in my group with that LIGHT, and many of you are, too. But no matter what their reasons for being Dream Killers, sometimes you have to leave them behind. Not only will it allow you to reach your dreams, it will inspire them to pursue their own!

There is nothing more unattractive than insecurity. You begin to feel awkward in the presence of your partner because you're conscious of their feelings of inadequacy. Over time, you find yourself over compensating for their lack of confidence.

But worst of all, insecurity changes the way you view them. Your vision of building a life together begins to fade because deep down inside you know there's no future with a person you can't be yourself with and who you don't respect.

~ Michael Baisden

Insecurity Is A Turnoff

Don't ever slow down from pursuing your dream just because your friends, family, or partner are insecure about your success! If they were meant to be in your life they will catch up! I always like to use the metaphor of a stick floating down a stream. I am the stick, the stream is my dream, and everyone on the bank of the river is standing on the sidelines. My attitude is, if you want to go with me you'd better jump in the water because I'm not getting out!

Sometimes it takes years to find your talent and passion, and it would be foolish to give it up or postpone it because someone in your life lacks the security to support you or the courage to pursue their own dream. Every day I receive e-mails from men and women who are on the verge of leaving their significant other because they are dealing with insecurity issues. Just this morning, while I was preparing to write this chapter, one of my Facebook friends sent me a frustrated e-mail asking why her boyfriend was suddenly trippin' over her success. The letter and my response are below.

> **Sarita wrote:** Good day Michael! Let me ask you a question or should I say your perspective. Why is it that a woman can be with a man who at first or maybe even sometimes for the first entire year will be so confident in himself but then he starts to have insecurity issues? I only ask because I tend to be having that issue not once but twice now. I am one of the most loyal women around, I don't flirt at all and I give my heart and my best. I'm very independent but not so independent that I don't let him do things for me. I strive for him to feel wanted or provide him with the sense that he is the man no matter how much I have or can do for myself, so why do men switch up on me like that? Please shine some light on this if you can.

> **My Response:** Sarita, men in general are not pro- grammed to handle today's woman — independent, out- going, ambitious thinkers and leaders. It's really not in our DNA, which is why when someone like you, who

is an entrepreneur, dreamer, thinker, doer and, might I add, attractive, it's a lot for a man to handle.

Short term it's all about the sex and having a nice arm piece, but over time, men see the potential of a woman and begin to ask themselves, "Do I fit into her future?" You're not the same woman you were last year, your energy attracts like-minded people who are also doers, thinkers, dreamers, etc., so I can just imagine who else has gravitated into your universe. Regardless if you're reacting to them or not, things are happening in your life and he notices it.

Unfortunately, you cannot manage someone else's insecurity. His self-esteem issues come from "Self." All you can do is leave yourself open to discuss it and reassure him that you're there for the long haul. But you can't fix him, that's his job.

■ ■ ■

I receive letters similar to this one every week, from both men and women. The most passionate responses I received on this topic came after I posted this quote on Facebook:

Never, I repeat, "Never" date or marry someone with low self-esteem! All the love, great cooking, and ego boosting in the world will not save a relationship if your partner does not feel good about him or her self physically, intellectually, financially and sexually.

Please stop with the Fix-A-Chick and Fix-A-Dude Mentality. It doesn't work!

The responses I received were enlightening. I could have written another chapter just responding to some of this incredible feedback.

> **Lynette wrote:** Insecure people will destroy themselves and the relationship in the process. Because their feet are grounded in fear so they kill possibilities!

> **Kevin wrote:** Michael this is such a good topic to write on. From my experience when in a relationship with someone that's insecure the relationship suffers tremendously. That deeper level of love is never attained because one resents the other for the insecure acts such as jealousy, lack of self-confidence, etc. Neither person truly loves with God's love because of the emotional turmoil that's brought into the relationship.

> **Tammy wrote:** Insecurity is like a cancer that can spread to all other aspects of a person's emotional stability. And inadvertently into any relationships they hold. There can be very little trust, honesty, or real communication. All core components to a successful relationship are destroyed because the other person walks on eggshells for fear of hurting the insecure person.

> **Robert wrote:** An insecure person will never feel loved no matter what you do or say. They will constantly

question your sincerity, loyalty, and genuine love because they don't love themselves.

Tea wrote: Insecurity is a direct result of immaturity of one of the partners in a relationship, married or not, brought on by some life event such as cheating, poor financial management, secrets and lies. Men and women need to be honest with themselves (even if this means getting counseling), come clean to his or her life partner about the feelings, develop a plan of action, implement that plan and deal with the results (even if this means leaving the relationship).

Melina wrote: I was just dumped by a man who accused me of being a liar and cheater, which I am not. His take is: I have too many men texting me and I am too friendly to those around me. I am actually a business banker and a Chair of a professional association. The men who text me are usually clients, prospects, or colleagues asking about anything they can come up with!!!! I breathed, ate, dreamt of my man and no one else... His insecurities took the best of him. Not fair; however, I know there is someone out there that can love and respect me, and my career. His loss.

■ ■ ■

In Melina's situation, I believe she already knew her relationship with this man didn't stand a chance. I know it hurts to lose someone you love, but his issues had nothing to do with her.

It's the things that people know deep down about themselves that make them insecure; it usually has nothing to do with the other person. His leaving was his way of communicating to her that he was not willing or able to deal with his issues. Receive it that way!

Liars, Cheaters
and Victims

Cheating is not a game, especially for the person being cheated on. Not only is it humiliating, it destroys self-esteem and puts a person's health at risk.

Cheating is also lying, and that's childish and immature. And maybe that's the real problem; most people don't know when to grow up!

~ Michael Baisden

There's Nothing Worse Than A Liar!

When someone tells you they're not seeing other people, you shouldn't have to guess whether or not they're telling the truth. At the beginning of the relationship a simple question is asked: "Are you dating or having sex with other people?" It's a simple yes or no answer. If your answer is "no" then you are expected to live up to your word. It's called having integrity. But every day people look their partners straight in the eyes and lie to them knowing full well they have no intention of living up to their promise.

I have issues with people who can't tell the truth, especially about something as serious as being faithful. If you can't handle the responsibility of a committed relationship, stop playing with people's emotions and stop wasting their valuable time. Infidelity can leave scars that last a lifetime. And the closer to home the betrayal happens, the harder it can be to recover. Cheating with a co-worker is bad enough, but when it happens with a close friend or relative, it can be devastating. The thought of your best friend or brother-in-law smiling in your face while having sex with your partner behind your back will have you ready to choke the hell out of somebody! And to add insult to injury, it often happens in the same bed you sleep in every night. Now that's disrespectful!

Finding out that someone has lied to you about being faithful is hard to accept no matter what age you are, but when it happens in your 40s, 50s and even 60s, it can make you shake your head and wonder, "Do people ever grow up?" You would think that a grown man or woman over 40 would know better, but just because a person is older doesn't mean they're mature. Look around at all the grown men who are dressing like 20-year-olds, saggy pants and all. They drive with their windows rolled down in their cars blasting rap music. Many of them have the same mentality and use the same slang as teenagers. If you closed your eyes, you wouldn't know if you were listening to someone's grandfather or a high school freshman.

Women over 40 can be just as immature. They gossip all day about the same issues as their daughters; they listen to the same music, watch the same reality TV shows and wear the same clothes. And some of them have taken being a cougar too far when they start dating young men in the same twenty-something age group. The Internet is full of stories about a mother and daughter duking it out over the same man, sometimes to the point of one killing the other. Now that's what I call having issues!

There should be a distinction between children and adults, mentally, conversationally, musically and as it relates to fashion. I'm not suggesting that women over 40 should dress like old maids, but is it asking too much to dress age appropriately? What does this have to do with cheating, you ask? Everything!

Cheating usually begins with physical attraction, which leads to the decision to cheat, and then the act of cheating. Mature adults understand that physical attraction is just that, it's an attraction; that doesn't mean you tear off your clothes and jump on top of the other person. That shows a lack of maturity. Dr. Gwendolyn Goldsby Grant, author of *The Best Kind of Love*, said it best: "Your erection is not an emergency!" As you mature, you learn to appreciate the beauty in other people and leave it at that. Maturity also means considering the consequences of your actions before you act, not afterwards. It's not just about STDs, unplanned pregnancies and getting caught; the real damage is the humiliation you put your partner through when your dirt comes out, and it always does sooner or later. How would you like it if your partner was screwing some strange man or woman and everybody knew about it but you? It's not a good feeling, is it?

Lying also breaks down a person's character. This is what keeps many of our men from reaching their full potential as leaders in politics, the community and in their households. Integrity is the most powerful tool you have in becoming successful and respected. How many men reading this book right now can stand up in the middle of a crowded room with everyone from their recent past in attendance and speak the truth about who they are, how they conduct their business, who they're involved with, and what kind of parent they are? Can you speak that truth without someone standing up and calling you a liar? When you can stand in front of a room, with a live microphone or on national television and speak the truth to people's faces, that's power!

We have to stop promoting this player's mentality to our young men, which is really nothing more than a mask to hide our in-securities. Real men tell women straight up from day one, this is who I am, this is who I'm involved with, this is the kind of relationship I'm interested in, and leave it up to the woman to decide whether or not to continue the relationship. That's a man!

It's not just the dirt we did when we were in our teens and 20s that drags us down but the games many of us continue to play in our 40s, 50s and 60s. It's a damn shame that even later in life the principle of being honest still doesn't exist for many men. And the confusing part about it for me is that men have so many more options than women when it comes to dating, getting married or having sex partners. Maybe not as many options as women think, but we have plenty of choices. So when I hear stories about unmarried single men cheating, I slap myself on the forehead and scream, "Why, fellas, why!?" We have all the choices in the world, and all we have to do is communicate to a woman that we're seeing other people. What's so complicated about that? For me it boils down to respect. I need to be able to walk into a room with women from my past and not have them pointing at me saying, "There goes that cheating dog!"

Likewise, women have to stop lying to their men about being monogamous when they know they are having sex and giving their time to other men. I'm sure there are plenty of guys who are willing to date and have sex with a woman even if she's involved with other men. So what's with the lies and secrets? We need to round up all the lying, whorish men and women and set up a website where they can lie and play games with each other so the rest of the grown-ups can get down to the business of building real relationships. I think I'll call it www. sloppystupidcheaters.com.

■ ■ ■

There's nothing worse than a cheater because cheaters ruin marriages and destroy the self-esteem of the people they cheat on. And the sad part about it is that cheaters most often don't even know why they're cheating. How many times have you seen these knuckleheads on talk shows and when they're asked, "So, why did you cheat?" their response is, "I don't know!" Well, the truth is most people who cheat really *don't* know why they do it. They have been lying for so long that telling the truth is not even an option. In their minds the lie is the truth. So let me set the record straight: Cheaters are shallow, they lack confidence, and they are masters at hiding their insecurities.

When I interviewed women who have dated these over-masculine, muscle-bound, so-called ladies' men, I discovered that these men were some of the most sensitive and insecure people you'll ever meet. In public they're confident, strong and take charge, but when it comes to dealing with emotions, they, like most men, are inept. And because men are afraid of becoming vulnerable, they create back-up relationships just in case they get dumped, cheated on, or the woman makes too many demands. But all this does is prevent him from creating deeper emotional bounds, which is what the objective of a healthy relationships is all about. Loving a woman is one thing, opening yourself up to getting your heart broken is another matter all together, especially if he's been hurt before. As I said, men can be more sensitive than women when it comes to dealing with emotions.

The other truth is that most men don't have the resources to attract and maintain a quality woman, so they create several relationships with women of lower caliber to compensate. Trust me, I've seen this process played out my whole life and I know what I'm talking about. Think about it. If you were a confident man who truly felt you had options, why would you lie to a woman about being monogamous? I'm not even referring to a married man who has his own set of issues because of the commitment he made on paper, but what possible excuse does the single cheater have? He's single, for goodness sake! Not God!

The insecurity factor is most obvious when men want to exercise their freedom to see other women but want to take away that same freedom from the woman. That's insecurity, not greed! A man who is greedy can have as many women as he wants, but once that greed turns into a lie about being monogamous to keep the woman from exercising that same option, it becomes a control issue. This is why I tell women not to fall into the trap of arguing about monogamy, but instead challenge the man on the principle of fair play. Instead of threatening him to not cheat or else, which doesn't work anyway, remind him that two can play at that game. Remember, ladies, you have options, too, and don't you dare give them up until you're sure he's holding up his end of the bargain. What's good for the goose is good for the gander.

Besides, the argument that some men and women make about monogamy is irrelevant. People kill me when they try to justify their cheating by saying, "It was only sex" or "Monogamy isn't natural." My response is, monogamy isn't the issue, it's about honesty. If you truly believe that being sexually exclusive to one person isn't in your nature, then be honest about it from day one! Don't take away your partner's right to choose whether or not to be in a three-way relationship. Not only does it lack integrity but it can also get you seriously hurt! And that will be an issue you brought on yourself.

The problem with forgiveness is that there is no "quick fix." You must exercise patience and work at repairing the damage. Don't expect the relationship to be the same because it never will be. Nor should it be. Your relationship should be different, better and stronger.

But if you feel in your heart that you cannot truly forgive, stop punishing yourself and your partner and move on! Otherwise, you will always see him/her as "the person who hurt you, lied to you and humiliated you." Be honest with yourself today and make a decision to work it out or move on.

~ *Michael Baisden*

After The Affair, Who's To Blame?

What would you do if you found out your partner had cheated? Most people would react by cursing out their partner, packing up their belongings and storming out the door. In the case of married couples, the decision might be to drag the cheating spouse through court and make their lives a living hell! Both reactions are typical — when someone has been hurt and humiliated so badly, sometimes all you want is to get revenge! But those reactions are based purely on emotions and can sometimes multiply the issues you already have, especially if there are children involved. I realize that betrayal is painful. It's hard to imagine that the person you loved and trusted could do such a thing. But after you calm down, you must consider the real-life implication of what you do next. There are factors that must be taken into consideration, such as making sure your finances are in order, keeping a roof over your head, minimizing the impact on your children, if there are any, and most importantly, assuring your emotional wellness.

And the best way to "get well" is not by confronting your cheating partner — that should wait until you calm down — but by doing some self-evaluation! Start by asking yourself, "What responsibility do I have in what happened? What can I learn from this? And what's the best way to move forward that will serve everyone's best interests, especially those of the children?" I already know what you're thinking: It's easier said than done! But whoever said this was going to be easy? And the toughest challenge in the process of moving forward is accepting that although everyone is responsible, no one is to blame.

Yes, your partner is responsible for cheating; yes, the person he or she cheated with is responsible for participating; and yes, you are responsible, too, for accepting the cheating, ignoring the signs or neglecting your spouse. And if none of these issues applies to you, then you are still responsible for what you do next. But pointing fingers and blaming your partner, or the person they cheated with, won't change anything. And blaming yourself won't make you feel any better, either. All blame does is feed into your anger, destroy your self-esteem and cloud your judgment, whereas focusing on "response-ability" gets to the root of the problems and teaches you something about your partner as well as yourself.

At some point in the relationship your partner chose to "Respond" to his or her attraction to another person by having sex or by emotionally cheating. He/she was not "Able" to make the proper judgment, which means he/she was Ir-Response-Able, or not responsible. It's possible to have a constructive conversation about your partner's lack of response-ability, whereas blaming someone is a never-ending argument that resolves absolutely nothing! Stay with me because this is important.

Whether you choose to leave the relationship or rebuild it, you have to address the issues of irresponsibility, which include poor judgment, lack of character, immaturity and dishonesty. Those are concrete issues that can be discussed, analyzed and decided on. All "Blame" does is say, it's your fault not mine. That doesn't accomplish anything! This attitude of "Blaming" is precisely why we have so many unresolved issues when our relationships end. The hurt person would rather blame the other person than fix the underlying problems or, at the very least, take away a valuable lesson that could help him/her in future relationships. I mean, what's the point in investing all those years and going through all that pain if you're not going to take something positive away from it? That's not intelligent.

But our biggest challenge is not moving past blame or even forgiving the person who betrayed us; sometimes the hardest thing to do is to forgive ourselves for making such poor decisions and for not following our instincts in the first place. At some point we have to take responsibility for volunteering to become victims.

Love is a beautiful thing! It can make you feel alive, like anything is possible. But love can also blind you to the reality of who a person truly is.

The truth is that, more often than not, we know when someone is not right for us, but instead of trusting our instincts we dive in with our eyes wide shut!

~ Michael Baisden

Eyes Wide Shut

There's always that moment that you reflect back on when you knew something wasn't quite right. Sometimes it's a subtle thing your partner says or does that raises an eyebrow. Meanwhile, that alarm goes off inside your head saying, "Run for Your Life!" Okay, maybe it's not always so dramatic, but you know what I mean, right? That's called your instincts. The question is, why do we constantly ignore them? Each time we do, we pay a price.

Love can do that to you; it can make you believe the impossible is possible. It alters reality. Love can make you see potential where there is none. It changes unacceptable habits into tolerable ones and makes you believe you're compatible with someone when you're not. Love is so powerful that it can make you ignore the advice of your friends, your family and your own instincts telling you this person is not right for you, and yet you move them into your home, buy them a car, pay off their debt, take care of their children and put up with abuse. That's how powerful love is. Or as Sade put it in her song, "Love Is Stronger Than Pride."

But is it just love that causes people to do insane things? Sometimes that's all it takes. But most often it's a combination of love, desperation, dependency, loneliness and low self-esteem; throw in being horny, and that's a lethal combination. One of the best interviews I did on this topic was with a lady from Houston named Lisa. Let me warn you in advance this story was one of the more extreme cases of being blinded by love. It not only cost her a broken heart, but also something much more precious: the safety of her child.

Lisa's Story: Fix-A-Dude

I'm telling my story in the hopes it will help another woman from going through the hell I just went through. They say that God never gives you more than you can bear but I'm beginning to question that theory because no one should have to suffer the way I did just for loving someone. But I guess that's how most women are, we buy into this fantasy that all we need is love and we can pray for the strength to get through the rest. But what we should be praying for is the common sense to make the right decision.

Well, for five years I prayed for a man to come into my life who would accept me and my daughter, and one day while I was at a weekend film festival, Gary came along. When I first saw him, I wasn't too interested, but as the night went on I warmed up to him. He had a great sense of humor. By the way, ladies, that's one of the traps we have to be careful of. A man will have you laughing all the way to the bank.

Anyway, he was all the things I asked for on my little wish list: just the right height, muscular, light brown eyes, and he was romantic. We exchanged numbers, and when I got back to Houston, he flew in from Los Angeles to visit. The first time was very cordial; we had dinner in the Galleria area and caught a movie, and later we had drinks at a bar near the Galleria, all his treat. I was impressed. But what I didn't realize was this was all a setup.

He flew in another three times, all expenses on him. The last time I allowed him to stay in one of my spare bedrooms because my daughter, who was 15, was staying at a girlfriend's house for the weekend. But as time went on, I began noticing he would start dropping hints about needing investors for a film project he was working on. I didn't think much of it at first since the short film he premiered at the festival had won a second-place award. I figured he was established, with all the wining and dining and jet-setting to and from Houston. Again, it was all just a setup.

To make a long story short, after two months of dating he talked me into moving him in so he could save money on travel and could work on his film projects. I didn't know it until the day he moved in that he wasn't shipping a car or furniture. All he had were two large suitcases and a garment bag. But by then I was committed and all my girlfriends were crazy about him. That's another trap, allowing yourself to be influenced by your horny, single girlfriends. My married friends were telling me to slow down while my desperate single ones were encouraging me to step out on faith. As it turned out, it was more like stepping on the plank of a pirate ship.

Three months and $10,000 of my savings later, there were still no film projects, not even a screenplay. That's when I started going online and doing my research. Come to find out the film that won the award was written, produced and directed by someone else. The only credit this fool had was as the illustrator for the DVD jacket. I was livid. I was going to throw him out, but by then he had developed a close relationship with my friends, my neighbors and my daughter. He was real smooth, he knew just how to get in and stay in. And I probably would have kept falling for it if it weren't for the one time I doubled back from work because I had left the portfolio for my presentation at home. When I walked into the house, I could hear the television on in my bedroom, which was odd because Gary never watched TV in bed; he was always in the den where he could watch the sixty-inch flat screen. When I walked in, I couldn't believe my eyes. The grown-ass 40-year-old man was buck-naked on top of my 15-year-old daughter. I screamed so loud I know the whole block must have heard me. I get sick to my stomach every time I think about it.

I pulled him off her and started beating both their asses with my fists. I know she was still a child, but she was old enough to know better. And as for Gary, the police are still searching for him to this day. Not surprisingly, I found out later that she wasn't the first child he had molested and I wasn't the first sucker to fall for his game. If there is a moral to this story, it's not to confuse desperation with love. I was turning 40, lonely, a little overweight, and I wanted a man around to show me affection and protect my child and me. But instead, my low self-esteem attracted a criminal who took more from me than I can ever get back.

■ ■ ■

Lisa's story is more common than you think. I have dozens of stories from women and men who have been through this kind of hell. We start out with good intentions to help out the person we love. We brush them off and get them back on their feet, hoping they'll reach their full potential so we can live happily ever after. But too often our need for love, companionship, validation, sex or whatever it is we're lacking costs us more than time and a few dollars. In Lisa's case it was $10,000 and her daughter's innocence, but for another gentleman I interviewed named Nick, it was a case of getting cleaned out. Literally!

Nick's Story: Fix-A-Chick

I have a degree in engineering, I own three homes, and I'm the head of my department at a well-known energy company, so I guess you can call me an educated fool! That's exactly what I feel like after what I put myself through. Notice, I put the blame on me because that's where it squarely belongs.

I know that most people blame the person who took advantage of them, but not me. I was the one who put myself out there. And although no one deserves what I had done to me, I'm not surprised. I met Stacie online. The first sign was her user name, which I can't mention without getting myself sued. But it was similar to something like ballin'diva. It was the kind of profile name that should have been a warning light for a man in my position. But like the song "Poison" by Bell Biv DeVoe said, "I fell for the big booty and smile."

Stacie was almost perfect, at least physically. She had a couple of kids, but the fathers were not in their lives. She had one child by her ex-husband and another by some guy she met two years later. And she was working part time as a model and a waitress at night. And that's where we decided to have our first date, at the bar she worked at downtown on Michigan Avenue. She wanted to feel me out in a safe environment, and I wanted to be able to run if she didn't look like her photos online. When I saw her in person, I wasn't disappointed. She was more attractive in person. She had long black hair that was midway down her back, dark eyes, a small waist you could almost wrap one hand around, and hips that curved out just right. We had been chatting for weeks online and on the phone, so when we finally had a chance to talk face-to-face, it was like we had known each other for years. It was obvious the attraction was mutual, and as time passed we became companions, inside and out of the bedroom.

Fast forward two months. I decided she was a keeper. That meant more public dates to upscale restaurants, company events, a meeting with the family, etc. That's when I went into Mr. Fix-It mode. I saw that she had a tacky nail job, so I referred her to a friend who was a great technician; her clothes were not up to my standards so I took her shopping at the Water Tower; her breasts were a little saggy after giving birth to her last child, so I paid for a boob job. Of course she had to be in the best shape so I paid for a membership at Bally's. I even ordered self-help books from amazon.com and had her watching MSNBC and CNN to get her more cultured. I was going for the complete makeover. But to Stacie's credit, she never asked for any of this, she just quietly went along for the ride.

By the time this transformation was complete, the babies' daddies popped back up in the picture. Not one but both of them. Now, all of a sudden, they wanted to spend time with their kids. I guess they figured she had hit the jackpot and wanted to stay close to the money, and one day the father of the youngest child, who had been in and out of jail, came by my house while I was out of town and cleaned me out. He stole my flat screens, computers and iPad, and he took all my tailor-made suits. All total, he cost me over $30,000. But here's the worst part, she was at my house while all of this was happening.

When I asked her why she didn't call the police, she said, "That's my child's father. I didn't want to see him go back to prison." I damned near hit the roof. "I told you not to let him pick up the kids from here!" I shouted at her. "He never would have known where I lived. And

I told you not to let anyone in while I was gone. I buy you clothes, shoes, toys for your kids, and these breasts you're wearing." Her response was cool and direct. "And I told you I never asked for any of this stuff," and then she calmly walked out the door with her two kids, a suitcase full of expensive clothes, and the two breasts that I had paid for.

Am I mad at her? The answer is no, but it's going to take me a long time to forgive myself for being such an idiot!

■ ■ ■

Whether it's because of love, lust or loneliness, both men and women make bad choices about who to give their hearts to and who to trust. Sometimes the best thing to do is take time out from relationships and just enjoy being single. The problem with that is that women, more so than men, feel pressured by friends and family to be in a relationship. They're in a no-win situation. If they get married and the guy is a jerk, they suffer, and if they decide not to date and be alone, then there's something wrong with them.

And that's another one of my issues. Why do married people treat being single like a disease? Single people don't need therapy, they don't need a shot, and they don't need sympathy. This may come as a surprise to a lot of married folks and people in relationships, too, but some people actually enjoy being single!

The Single Life

People are single for many reasons. Some are enjoying their lives until a worthy person crosses their path. Others are too busy with kids, sick parents, school, etc. But the main reason why most healthy and mature adults are single is because they refuse to compromise their standards; they simply don't have time or energy to put up with games and other nonsense.

~ Michael Baisden

Being Single Is Not A Disease

The reaction of most men when they meet an attractive single woman is, "What's wrong with you?" But my question is, why does something have to be wrong? Why is it so unbelievable that an attractive woman would choose not to be in a relationship? Maybe the reason she's single is because there *isn't* anything wrong with her. People can be very toxic, and they bring a lot of baggage from previous partners. The fact that a person who has many options is not in a relationship speaks to his or her high self-esteem, not their lack of it. It's easy to just jump into a situation with someone and start calling him or her your man or woman. But it takes discipline and knowing your self-worth that makes it easy to wait on someone who will uplift you and not bring you down.

Roni C. wrote: I personally find that I am happiest single. My life is drama free. My bills are paid. I don't need to check in with anyone. I'm not concerned with what anyone else is doing. I'm comfortable going to the movies alone or going out to eat alone. If I want, I can definitely date when I choose, so that is never a problem. I am just comfortable in my own skin. I'm just happy!

■ ■ ■

"Amen, Roni," I'm clapping at my computer. That's precisely the attitude every single man and woman should have. Most people have never taken themselves out on a dinner and movie date, and enjoyed doing it! And that's a shame. What you do demonstrates the love you have for your own company and for yourself. That attitude is precisely what attracts healthy people into your universe.

Besides, being in a relationship or marriage is not an indicator that a person is emotionally healthy or even happy. I hear more complaints from so-called happily married people than single people. That's not an attack on marriage; I'm just stating my experience. It's surprising that a woman would even have to defend being single, especially to other women, but women are often the ones applying the most pressure.

Carol J. wrote: It never fails, every holiday, birthday and graduation, my mother puts me on blast in front of the entire family, "When are you going to get married and give me some grandbabies?" I got so fed up one Christmas I responded, "If you want some babies so badly, adopt one!" I'm sick and tired of women feeling as if our only purpose on earth is to find a man and procreate. I swear, we women are our own worst enemy.

■ ■ ■

Carol is right, and the more attractive and successful the woman is, the more she has to explain why she isn't barefoot, pregnant and living in a house with a white picket fence. Whose reality is that anyway?

But attractive and successful men get similar treatment, sometimes worse. Recently, I posted a request for single men to submit their photos and status on my networking site, Minglecity.com. Several handsome men posted photos and detailed profiles. Some were doctors, lawyers, cops, etc. But instead of the women engaging them about their careers or trying to hook up, they started grilling them about why they were single and accused them of being gay! One gentleman who is a doctor in his 40s was called selfish because he wasn't sharing his success, which basically meant he wasn't sharing his money!

My response was, "Wow, did I miss something? Is there some unwritten rule that says if you look a certain way, reach a certain age or earn a decent paycheck, you must follow the dotted line to the wedding chapel?" Well, here's breaking news for the "What's wrong with you?" crowd: Millions of people are perfectly happy being single, and they're not gay, crazy, selfish or damaged, and even if they are one or more of those things, at least they're honest enough to admit they aren't ready to be in a relationship!

A perfect example is my own post on Baisden Live on Facebook. I was asked by one of my friends why I was still single. My response was, "I'm not at a point in my life where I'm ready to share my hectic lifestyle and sporadic schedule with another person. To have a successful relationship you must be willing to make that special person a priority. Right now, my career is my priority."

Boy, did they let me have it! One woman accused me of being afraid of commitment. Another said I was making excuses for not settling down. And the most humorous of all was that I must be gay. Let me get this straight, if a man or woman chooses not to be in a committed relationship or get married, they are irresponsible, selfish or gay. Really? My manager, who is a woman, once told me, "Women want to hear the truth until it's something they don't want to hear." I think that's probably true of people in general.

But the truth is what it is. Mature single adults know that relationships are huge responsibilities and they want no part of it. Relationships require an investment of time, money, energy and emotions, and you must be accountable for your comings and goings. And that's just the beginning. You must also be willing to compromise and put someone else's needs before your own. You must be willing to accept everything about them, from their children to their financial situation, their habits, issues with their health, and put up with their family and friends.

When you're in a relationship, you will be impacted by every issue your partner has experienced from birth until the day they met you, whether it's abandonment issues, baggage from previous relationships, abuse, diseases or bad credit. You don't get to pick and choose which parts of the person to love ... it's all or nothing! Relationship by definition means to connect to another human being. That means connecting to your partner's dreams and aspirations as well as their unresolved issues.

I always like to emphasize this point about relationships: As you mature, the key is not figuring out what you want, but what you don't want! Single people are just being upfront by saying, "I don't want to be in a relationship!" They should be applauded for their honesty. We need to stop pressuring people to be in something they don't want to be in.

I saved the best for last. Thomas J.'s comment is the perfect one to end this chapter.

> **Thomas wrote:** You really don't appreciate being single until you've spent a few years in a bad marriage. When you finally get divorced you feel like you've been released from prison — talk about *Shawshank Redemption*. There's nothing like having the ability to do what you want to do and come and go as you will! I'm never giving up that freedom again. I don't mean to put down marriage, but too often when you say "I do,"

people think they own you or they become your mother or father. It's easy to understand why the divorce rate is so high; most of the people who get married never enjoyed their own freedom as a single person so they have no problem trying to take yours away. My advice is to stay single for as long as you can, and if you do settle down, do it with someone who is happily single. As you said in one of your quotes, Michael, "How can you be happily married if you're not happily single first?"

We all have issues, but sometimes those issues are so severe they get in the way of developing healthy relationships. But the biggest problem isn't fixing it; the challenge is making people realize they have issues in the first place.

~ Michael Baisden

Some People
Are Better Off Single

Some people have entirely too much baggage to be involved in a relationship. They need to be still, unpack, take time out, re-evaluate, heal, chill and avoid relationships like the plague. "Bag Ladies" or "Garbage Men," as I like to refer to them, have no business dating, getting married or having close intimate ties with other human beings. They are angry, jaded, negative, prejudiced, toxic, and it's always the other person's fault that it didn't work out. Candice posted this story about being a bag lady.

Candice wrote: When I first heard Erykah Badu's song "Bag Lady," I thought she had written that song just for me. I was carrying around so much hate for my ex-husband that I couldn't see straight. Anything that reminded me of him was a trigger: smelling his cologne, driving by our favorite restaurant, sitting in traffic next to the same car he drove. Even hearing his name out in public would set me off, and his name was Bill — how common can you get? Any man who was unfortunate enough to cross my path was in for a 30-minute rant about no-good men.

Some of the good ones thought they could change my attitude by showering me with gifts and compliments, but I was so far gone, Denzel Washington could have asked me out on a date and I would have thought he was a dog! Looking back, there was nothing that any man could have done to make me feel better about myself or about men. I needed time to work on myself. It has taken three years and I'm still not ready to date. My advice to any man who meets a woman who is carrying emotional baggage is, Run Forrest Run!

■ ■ ■

I had to laugh at Candice's honesty. She knew she was a mess and was in no condition to deal with the emotions of another relationship. Moving on from that kind of pain is not easy. She admitted it had been three years for her, but for some women it has taken over seven years to recover emotionally, mentally and financially. Relationships can also take a financial toll. I've heard stories about entire life savings being tapped out.

One man called into my radio show on the topic of paternity fraud. He had just discovered that another man fathered the son he had raised for 10 years. And to make matters worse, he was forced to continue to pay child support until the child was 18, even though the mother admitted the child wasn't his. Now how long do you think he's going to need before he can trust and love again?

But carrying baggage is only one of many reasons why some people are not ready for a committed relationship. Another one is selfishness, or the inability to compromise. That means not always getting to have things your way, and that can be a big adjustment, especially for people who have lived alone for a number of years. The expression most often used is "Being Set in Your Ways," but I like to refer to it as "The All About Me Mentality." I want to go here, I don't want to eat there, I raise my children my way, I don't like those kind of movies, I go where I want when I want! I, I, I! These people live in their own little bubble where everything centers on them.

> **Donna wrote:** I have no one to blame but myself. When I met my husband, he told me on day one, "It's all about me!" I mean, he literally said those exact words. The first sign was when he never stopped working to take me out to dinner or the movies. Then it was coming home late after playing golf when he knew I had plans for us

to spend some alone time. But the light-bulb moment was when he became selfish in the bedroom. Now mind you, I had no reason to believe he was cheating; it was a gradual slacking off. First the foreplay stopped, then the longevity stopped, then the passion stopped. I'll never forget one night I was watching *The Color Purple* when Celie was describing what is was like having sex with Mister. She said it felt like he was going to the bathroom on her. I burst out in tears because that's exactly how I felt. No passion, no connection, no love, no nothing! Now add all that to the other things he wasn't doing and I knew it was time to go.

But again, I don't blame him. He told me upfront that it was his world, and everything he did reflected his words. And like a big dummy I thought I was going to transform him with my incredible love. We women have a tendency to do that. Since that relationship I've learned to look for those same traits in other men. If a man isn't considerate and willing to do the little things that it takes to make me happy, I head for the hills! Because if he's not doing those little things in the beginning of the relationship, he's damn sure not going to do them later.

■ ■ ■

Donna's story is more common than you think. Too often men like her ex-husband get involved in relationships and end up robbing women of a chance at true companionship and creating another bitter woman. Relationships require people to be considerate, unselfish and most importantly, consistent. That goes for giving gifts, going out on dates, calling to say goodnight, staying in shape, making yourself up, sending flowers and being adventurous in the bedroom. There is nothing worse than being with a man or woman who starts something and then doesn't finish it!

But guess what? People who are selfish and inconsistent have every right to be that way. There's nothing wrong with having a selfish mentality if you want to remain single. But if you think you're going to be getting into a relationship with that attitude with a person who knows their self-worth, you have another thought coming.

Do You Have Room For A Relationship?

Some people are single because they haven't made room in their lives for a relationship. And when I say made room, I mean that literally. Do you have room in your closet, do you have room in your drawers, do you have room in the medicine cabinet, do you have room in your schedule? How can we expect someone of quality to be attracted to us when we design our whole lives to fit only us? We live in just enough space to fit in *our* stuff; we only have enough space in our schedule for *our* friends, kids, family, work, church and maybe the gym. Emotionally, we're invested in our friends and their issues. And then we have the audacity to ask, why am I not meeting any quality single men or women? My answer is, you don't have room for one!

People are working longer hours to make ends meet, there's homework with the kids, three to four hours of sports or reality TV every night, Facebook and Twitter take up another hour or two a day, and let's not forget the hour-long phone conversations and texting with friends gossiping about absolutely nothing! So why are you so surprised that you're single? You don't deserve a good man or a good woman! They require your time!

And for the ladies, I need you to write this next lesson down and share it with all your girlfriends. Men do not, will not, never have and never will date a woman who is unavailable. They may stick around for a month or two if you're attractive and the sex is good, but after that, they'll be gone like a puff of smoke. *Poof!* It may be a badge of honor to be a mover and shaker in corporate America, but in a man's world, it's a deal breaker!

But here's the interesting part: Most of those men and women who are too busy or unwilling to make space in their closets, in their drawers and in their schedules are most often the ones who wind up in affairs with men and women who are married. You don't have to worry about them taking up your busy schedule or valuable space; they have plenty of closet and drawer space at home with their spouses and children. All they need is a chair to drape their underwear over for their Friday night booty call.

When you limit your emotional, mental and physical space, you're projecting part-time energy into the universe, and you'll get back exactly what you deserve — a part-time lover. I've said it once, and I'll say it a thousand times, Karma is real!

Kinda Single

I have a question. Is a person considered single if he or she has a casual sex partner they see regularly, even if that partner is married or in another relationship? If so, how do you explain that to a prospective partner? When they ask, "Are you in a relationship?" how do you respond? Do you omit by saying, "No, I'm single" and leave it at that? Or do you give full disclosure and say, "Yes, I'm single but I'm having sex two or three nights a week with the same partner." The honest response is the full disclosure because if you're having consistent sex with the same person over a period of time, you're not single, you're "Kinda Single."

Not to mention you're creating a bond with that person and one or both of you is more emotionally involved than you're willing to admit. It's easy for the lines to get blurred between what is a casual and what is a committed relationship, mainly because the act of sex itself is a serious act for most people. And the better the sex is, the stronger the bonds. Most people get so caught up in the act of sex, the orgasms and the intimacy that they forget they are in a sexual relationship that's supposed to be temporary. When a new person comes along and one of the parties wants to pursue a monogamous relationship, those bonds have to be broken, and they can be just as difficult to break for men as they are for women.

83

This sex question is a dilemma for many single adults, especially women. "Do I satisfy my sexual needs until I find a significant other," they ask, "or do I save myself?" Some of you are probably laughing to yourselves and thinking, save myself for what? Most women are learning to use men for sex the same way men use women, and some of them are better at it than us. But the question is, does having casual sex and being "Kinda Single" make you more or less likely to find someone who wants more than sex? It may not matter to you, but I can promise you it matters to us men.

I can't help but laugh when I hear men say, "Tell me the truth about who you're sleeping with. I won't judge you." Ladies, don't fall for the banana in the tailpipe or the Okie Doke. Most men cannot handle the truth about you having casual sex with other men, not if they see you as wife material or a potential serious girlfriend. I'm not telling you to lie, but based on the security level of the man, use your own discretion.

Men also have to address this issue of having casual sex. Mature men know there's no such thing, especially if the woman is exclusive to him and/or the sex is on a regular basis. There's always a price for sex, whether it's time, money or conversation to hear about how her day went. We all pay a price, the biggest being the possibility of missing out on a good thing because we're settling for the easy and familiar thing. When you give your time, energy and body to a person who is emotionally unavailable and/or doesn't meet your standards, it only moves you farther away from your ideal partner, not closer.

If you want a better chance at lifetime happiness, sometimes you have to let go of "in the meantime" satisfaction!

You should always take time out between relationships. Too often we jump from one relationship into the next without taking inventory of where we are mentally and emotionally. Even men are learning the value of time out!

How can you choose the right man or woman for YOU when you don't even know who YOU are?

~ Michael Baisden

Time Out!

Sometimes the best way to start a chapter is with someone else's voice. This is what a woman named Wendy wrote to me about the importance of time out:

> **Wendy wrote:** I'm taking time for me right now! First of all I'm healing my heart and filling my spirit! I understand that this time is needed to look at myself and evaluate things within myself. Right now I'm becoming the person I want to be! We wonder why we attract the same kind of men! We wonder where the mistakes were made. Saying yes too quickly can be a problem — yes to dating, yes to sex. If a man really wants you, he can wait to jump in the bed.

Birdie wrote: Michael, this is what they are saying; they have been catering to all the man's needs and they forgot to take care of self! That's what most nurturing women do.

■ ■ ■

As I'm reading these e-mails, I'm asking myself, "Don't men need time out, too?" I know I do. There have been times when I and other men I know needed to take a step back from all the expectations and drama that some women bring to the relationship. The truth is we all need a time out! Time out to re-evaluate, to balance our emotions, to heal, to detox, and time out to breathe!

Madelin wrote: During time out, you learn how to be honest with yourself and what makes me happy. Don't take yourself too seriously, laugh out loud and lots of inner peace. Last but not least, letting my hair down helped a lot, and learning how to please me and communicating to the other person how to please me.

Sandra S. wrote: What I am doing is getting to know me and be happy :) Yes I agree we women are emotional and can be desperate (I have done that, been there). But going on our emotions is not good because we aren't giving ourselves time to heal. We should do what makes us happy as women instead of constantly trying to please the other person and forget about ourselves because we're trying to find love. It is best to step back and reflect on what we want out of life. And most importantly, love yourself first!

■ ■ ■

The most common issue that must be addressed when taking time out is the importance of rebuilding self-esteem. The end of a relationship can be a traumatic experience, especially if it ended on a bad note, which they most often do, such as with infidelity, abuse or neglect. And no matter how much your friends or even the person who did you wrong tells you it was not your fault, it's human nature to blame yourself and begin overanalyzing yourself to the point of piling on to your own abuse.

And it only hurts more when that person who meant the world to you can move on so easily, as if the relationship never even happened. Now that's adding insult to injury! So how do you move past that? It's been my experience that the best cure is time. And that's why "Time Out" is so critical. You can't start healing if you're constantly in the mess that's causing the damage. One suggestion to separate yourself emotionally from your former partner is called "Womb Work."

China wrote: For women it is very important to do what is called "womb work" after a relationship. This work helps with breaking the "soul tie" of the previous mate. This helps with baggage. Womb Work consists of various things such as: baths, meditation, tears, laughter, wine, workshops to name a few.

■ ■ ■

So, I'm wondering, what do we call the process for men? We need cleansing, too. Not surprisingly, whenever I posted about men taking time out, I rarely got a response, and they definitely don't call into my radio program where millions of women can listen in. And maybe that's why men have so many unresolved issues.

Most women don't know this about men, but we hurt longer and deeper than women do, and we're less likely to trust again. The truth that no man wants to admit is that we're more sensitive than women. I'm not talking about "crying at movies" sensitive, what I mean is, once a man gives his heart to a woman, he's all in, hook, line and sinker! And because we don't love that often, we don't have much experience at having our hearts broken. Once that happens, every woman he meets afterwards will have to pay for it! Women, on the other hand, have more emotional practice; they are allowed to cry, to hurt, to complain, and do it all publicly. It's socially accepted. So over time they become more emotionally resilient. Not to mention women are hopeless romantics — after every devastating disappointment there's always hope that the next man will be different.

So how do you know when it's safe to go back into the dating waters after the time out is over?

Averil wrote: I know I'm ready to get back into dating because I am happy being alone. I know what I want

and need from a man and I'm aware of my input in past
failed relationships. Before getting with someone else, I
needed to learn my strengths and weaknesses, to learn
that my happiness comes from within, not from a man,
to learn that having great expectations from my partner
is right up there with trying to change him. If I don't like
who he is, I don't need to be with him, period!

Michele F. wrote: You know you are ready to dive
back in the dating pool when you are no longer angry;
you have let the blame game go. You have stopped the
pity party, you don't mention his name every 4 seconds,
and have ceased and destroyed all physical evidence of
him. You are content to spend a Saturday night home
alone with a great glass of red wine, a great book and a
DVD and you are good with that. You are happy dining
out alone and don't feel lonely. You stop playing "Our
Song." You have accepted responsibility for your part
in the demise of the relationship and are ALERT as to
what you don't want in a union. You are basically happy
with YOU!

My response: Michele, I couldn't have ended this
chapter any better. Let's move on!

Happily Ever After?

Marriage begins with dating, and dating is a process of elimination! So if you discover that your partner doesn't meet your standards or share your values, even if it's the day before the wedding, don't you dare go through with it!

Apologize to your family and friends and tell your fiancé "no hard feelings," and then move on with your life! Remember, the only thing worse than a canceled wedding is a bad marriage.

And to hell with those people who call you picky. Be selective!

~ Michael Baisden

Rocket Love!
Why Are People Rushing
To The Altar?

Why is everyone in such a rush to get married? It doesn't magically change who you are; it doesn't improve your relationship; you don't love your partner any stronger, and besides, the couple is probably already having sex. So where's the emergency? Why do I feel as if alarms are going off all across this country to rush to bag a husband or a wife? Now let me be clear; I'm not saying that the institution of marriage isn't important, because it is. My question is, why do we seem to be rushing to get married? Why not take your time to get to know whom you're marrying. When I posted this issue on my Facebook page I received many different points of view. Some were mind-blowing!

Beth wrote: You can be with someone for 20 years and not know who your partner truly is. There's no guarantee that it will last if you wait six years or six weeks. I say go for it when you feel it's right, regardless of how soon it is.

Karen wrote: Whether it's sooner or later, both people know right away if they want to spend the rest of their lives together, so why wait!

Jacqueline wrote: The longer you wait, the more likely the man is to get comfortable and never want to marry you.

Samantha wrote: I would never shack up before marriage; why would any man buy the cow when he can get the milk for free? Yes, we've been sexual for years but moving in together is no different than being married. So if he wants goodies 24/7, he'll have to pay for it.

Lindsey wrote: My husband and I were married 3 months after meeting and dating and have been married 16 years. I admit we were older and beyond the childish BS stage. We did a lot of talking about our likes and dislikes. I met all of his family that was in our city. We communicated very well. As a matter of fact, we went to a couples' dinner. Some of the couples had been married over 25 years. We played a game to see who knew their spouses best. My husband and I won.

■ ■ ■

All I could say after reading these posts was, "Wow!" So this is what it has come to. I should launch a new website called GetMarriedRightDamnNow.com. Yes, marriage is important. Yes, I want people to have healthy long-term marriages. Yes, we need to promote marriage as an important institution in our community. But we need to slow the hell down! One woman responded to all this madness with a post that was not only honest, it was prophetic.

> **Carlotta wrote:** O Lord!!!! Please take MB's advice; otherwise there will be a tragedy! People who try to rush marriage are hiding something about themselves hoping you don't find them out too soon. The signs are there; besides, if it's For Life, what's the rush?

■ ■ ■

Bingo! That's exactly my point! If you're already having sex, financially stable, and you're confident in your love for one another, what's the rush ... unless you're hiding something or you don't want your partner to change his or her mind. First of all, let's do the math: If it took you 30, 40 or 50 years to find your "Soul Mate," why would you be concerned that he or she is going to suddenly bail out? If it's real, then put it to the test and get to REALLY know each other. That way there are no surprises down the line after we buy a house together or start having children.

Marriage is a big deal, and most people's attitudes seem to be "Let's just do it and God will work out the rest!" But is that intelligent, and is that the advice you would give someone who was considering marriage? I don't think so.

The woman who told the story about getting married after knowing her partner for only three months even suggested later in her post that younger couples should wait at least a year or more because they don't have as much life experience. But I think it should be the reverse. When you have lived a longer life, you might be more mature, but you also might have more skeletons, more baggage and, most importantly, more to lose. But even mature men and women can be blinded by love. In fact, sometimes the older you are, the more desperate you become. Even some 50-year-old women want to have "Their Day." The attitude seems to be "Common sense be damned!" They are determined to announce to the world like the character Shug in *The Color Purple*, "Izz-married now!"

And what is the motivation of a man who would make a life-time commitment to a woman he only knew for three months, or even six? Is it love at first sight? Or is he sick and in need of a nurse? Did he feel he met his soul mate? Or is his child support emptying his bank account? Is he a hopeless romantic? Or is he crazy? I don't mean to sound cynical; I want to see people get married and stay married, but three months? Really? One year is pushing it, but at least you go through four seasons together. And remember, this wasn't a case where they knew one another for years and then started dating. She was very specific in saying that they were married three months after they met. And my issue is not so much with that one example; it's with all the people who were perfectly fine with that short courtship. As one woman stated, "I think that's romantic."

Whatever happened to getting to know each other and having an engagement period? I guess that's just a waste of time, too. And where is the importance of marriage counseling in all of this madness? I don't care how much time you spend together talking, meeting family or even having a background check. There is no substitute for spending time with a person, not with his or her family, but going through some ups and downs together. And there are not enough ups or downs in three months or even six months. But we live in a fast-food society, so I guess this is an example of new drive-thru marriages. "May I take your order, please?"

By the way, the couple who married after dating for only three months have been happily married for 16 years and that's great for them! But this is not about them; it's about this frantic race to get to the altar "by any means necessary." Maybe it's because of the perceived man shortage, the bad economy, or maybe it really is about love. But if it's love, I mean true love, all I'm asking is, what's the rush?

Is It About The Wedding Or The Marriage?

For most people marriage is a sacred act. When they stand before the preacher and repeat the vows "For richer or poorer, through sickness and health, until death do us part," they have every intention of keeping them, and many do. The institution of marriage is not a game; it's a serious commitment.

But too many people confuse the ceremony with the actual marriage. In my opinion, being married to your partner happens long before your wedding day. It takes place in the heart and soul, not at the altar. The ceremony is the public announcement and the legal certification of your love for each other. I think that's an important distinction because far too often we put too much emphasis on planning elaborate events and spending tons of money mainly to show off to our friends and family.

What we should be focusing on is getting the marriage off to a healthy start. Now I'm not trying to rob women of having their big day; it's supposed to be an event with memories that last a lifetime. But keep in mind that the wedding only lasts one day, but debt and the problems it brings can last forever.

For the last three decades the No. 1 cause of divorce has been related to money. Why then would you start your marriage off by intentionally going into debt? That's just not intelligent. For those who can afford to splurge without worrying about taking out loans, maxing out credit cards or spending money that should be going towards a down payment on a house, I say go for it! Pop those bottles of Cristal and let the doves fly! However, the majority of people who plan big weddings find themselves already in huge debt before they can even say "I do!"

When I was ready to get married, I was working for the Chicago Transit Authority and my then-wife was working for a travel agency. We decided to keep our wedding simple. We spent five days in Las Vegas, stayed at a nice hotel, and exchanged vows at one of those quaint little chapels. I'll never forget how nervous she was. I thought she was going to pass out! All total we spent about $3,000. After the wedding and honeymoon were over, we went back to our everyday lives without a cent of debt. And although the marriage only lasted five years, we left as friends and money was never our issue. We came into the marriage with no debt, and we left with no debt.

So the question for every couple considering marriage is simple. "Is it about the ceremony or the marriage?" The stress of getting married is bad enough without adding more issues. All you need is a bride, a groom, the ring and a preacher, and you're set; everything else is extra. The couple have to decide in advance how many extras they can afford, like the cost of adding more people, extra travel for relatives, extra ballroom space, extra waiters, extra bartenders, which all means extra headaches.

But even as the bills continue to add up, the bride and groom can get so carried away with the excitement of the ceremony and being husband and wife that they lose sight of the reality that someone has to pay for all of it. What was once a simple gathering of close friends and family can quickly explode into an extravaganza that would rival the Grammys! And often the cost goes far beyond settling invoices and credit card statements. In too many cases, the marriage itself ends up becoming bankrupt, not just financially but emotionally.

Darlene's story is the perfect example of putting the ceremony before the marriage.

Darlene's Story: Bridezilla

Like most of my girlfriends I wanted to be married my entire life. Yeah, I played that strong and independent role and put up the façade of being a corporate business-woman determined to break the glass ceiling, but deep down inside all I wanted was to be married and raise a family. It's sad that I could never say that out loud around my family or friends. Your parents invest thousands of dollars into your education, sometimes mortgaging the house, and they expect you to do something with it. And that doesn't include changing diapers and being a housewife. And you definitely can't announce that to your friends, half of whom own their own homes and brag about how they don't need a man. These and other factors transformed me into a wedding monster, one I couldn't control or recognize until it was too late.

When you meet the right man, it's exciting and scary at the same time. At first you're guarded and pessimistic wondering when the jerk is going to reveal himself, but that never happens. Kevin was the perfect gentleman, hard-working, honest, established and no children, thank God! But what made him most attractive was he was a man who believed in marriage. His parents were married for 38 years, his grandparents had been together for 55 years, his two brothers were married — you get the picture. And after he discussed marriage, it wasn't one of those typical situations you hear about where the woman nags and practically begs the guy to get married; Kevin was consistent in his words and actions. He truly acted like he wanted to be married, no games, no mind changing; he was ready.

But here's the problem. I didn't love Kevin, not the way a wife should love a husband, and I knew there was a difference. But after a year of dating, he got down on his knee and proposed to me. And here's what complicated the situation: He did it in front of my girlfriends. I'm not even sure I would have said yes if it hadn't happened with them all sitting there watching. But there was no way I was going to tell this wonderful man "no" in front of that group, no way! So I did what any woman would do, I accepted.

My friends were all teary-eyed and full of congratulations. And they couldn't stop complimenting me on the fat diamond ring he put on my finger. That took the experience to a whole new level and would only add more pressure to my situation. They must have taken 50 pictures with that ring; I didn't know if it was my night or the ring's.

The next day after all the hoopla was over, Kevin left to play golf and I was home alone with my thoughts. "Am I really going to go through with this?" I asked myself while looking at my reflection in the bathroom mirror. At that moment, one of my girlfriends, Angie, called. When I picked up, three voices screamed simultaneously. They were so loud I thought my head was going to explode!

"Congratulations, Girl!" they yelled in unison.

"When is the big day?" Angie asked. "I know you're going to let me organize your ceremony. You know I'm good at putting together events."

"And I know the perfect photographer," Valerie added. "I can get him at a discount; he owes me a favor, if you know what I mean."

"I'll contact my cousin who is a manager at the Marriott. I'm sure he can get you a discount on the main ballroom," Rebecca added. "This is going to be fun!!!!!"

As I sat there listening to these women screaming in my ear, my head started to spin. "What have I gotten myself into?" I thought. "And who are these women?" It was almost as if they were living vicariously through me, which was shocking because none of them had ever expressed any interest in getting married. And then it dawned on me; they were hiding behind their titles and cars and houses just like me.

Suddenly I felt the pressure to not only go through with this wedding for myself but for them, too. And I couldn't bear the thought of backing out and being subjected to more male bashing for the next 20 years. So I did what any other red-blooded American woman would do; I ran up thousands of dollars of debt, let my inexperienced girlfriends control every aspect of the wedding, and I walked down the aisle and married a man who by then felt more like a good friend than a husband.

Now that we have a child, I hope I can grow to love him as a husband. If not, I can always get divorced. But at least I can say, I had my day!

■ ■ ■

After interviewing Darlene, I was left feeling a little depressed, not only for her but because I know there are thousands, if not millions, of men and women who get married to people they don't truly love every day. Some of them feel pressured by friends, family or circumstances, while others are just determined to be married, no matter what. They are determined to have their day and stand in front of the whole world and say, "Look at me, somebody loved me enough to marry me!"

■ ■ ■

I posted this question on my social media site, Minglecity.com, to get the perspective of my members. There were over 1,000 comments and 200,000 views. They commented on whether couples put more importance on the wedding than the marriage. However, the vast majority of the comments were about the ridiculous amounts of money people waste getting married. Share these comments with someone you know who is thinking about a big wedding. I think this might convince them to change their mind.

> **Angel wrote:** Why spend so much money for a wedding? You're only going to wear the dress once. Then half of the time the bride doesn't want to mess up the cake, but when they do eat the cake, there is a lot left over that ends up sitting in the fridge getting freezer burn. Plus flowers that will rot in the attic, invitation cards you can

make yourself. It's just too much! Weddings are for you and your mate to say how much you love each other in front of friends and family. Not for you to get all fancy and jazzy for one night to show the world that you are balling.

Jimmy wrote: I am a preacher and have seen many who have spent costly amounts on the wedding but quickly forget about the vows. I am always saying remember who is standing here at this altar, and I take time teaching the meaning of the banns and covenant. So while they are getting masks to portray like that's all, remember you still have to live when it's over and the masks come off and you have to pay the bills. Where is your support? While you were dreaming, they had already made up their minds that they weren't going to do either because they really didn't care for whom you chose or this fantasy and having them flip the bill. So my word is this to any and all who wish to get married: KEEP IT SIMPLE. IT WORKS FOR THE BEST! GOD BLESS.

Lovetta wrote: It's about the marriage. The ceremony is for one day. The marriage is for a lifetime. Have a wedding you can afford, not to impress people. Taking excessive debt into your marriage is ridiculous! Set financial goals for yourselves. Save up for your wedding and honeymoon. Go to marriage counseling to gain a better understanding of what marriage is and is not, and the communication skills to work towards developing a marriage that works for you as a couple.

Blu wrote: First pay off all your personal bills before you get married, don't take any debt into the marriage. To pay off your bills, divide them into 12 months and pay that amount every month until they are paid off! If you need more time, that's how long it needs to be before you get married. Second, plan to have the wedding you can pay cash for, and spend the most money on your honeymoon (marriage is about you and your spouse), invite the people who are the closest to you, who don't expect you to go over the top. They just want to see you happy and legal with that one. Put the money you save into an investment that will last you longer than a wedding, like a house, your rings (that can get you some cash later, when needed), or an account to pay future debt off that you two accumulate together. Third, only cash gifts from attendees, and use it to open up your joint account and moving expenses to move into the house you two will share. Rent the dress, like the guy rents the tux. Unless it's something you can alter and wear again, it's only wasted (that pass it down stuff won't work; your daughter will want her own).

Dorthann wrote: To that couple I would say this: Don't allow an expensive ceremony to dictate debt into the beginning of your future together as man and wife. The honeymoon may not last that long. It is natural to want a beautiful ceremony, but it should never be at the expense or cost of your own true happiness together. Being debt-free will give you and your loved one fewer sleepless nights and more romantic ones. Most of the time people come to judge what your ceremony will be like in the first place, then they go home with full bellies at your expense, and just talk about the negativity that they can find in the ceremony some more. Only your closest family and friends will truly be happy for you anyway.

Ellie wrote: STOP IT!!! STOP IT!! Stop focusing on all the foolishness, i.e., the party, the guests, the dress, the food, etc. None of that matters in a marriage. What matters is that you are both on the same page and willing to work as a team during the tough times as well as the good times because marriage is one of the toughest jobs you will ever do. So get your head out of the "fairytale BS" and focus on building a marriage that lasts based on trust, communication, integrity, love and respect. You also need a sense of humor in a marriage. Because the sex and love comes and goes, you have to be able to laugh at your mistakes and grow together.

Felecia wrote: If you are stressing over the expense of getting married, then that is what your marriage will be like for the rest of the time you are together and more than most, then you are getting married for the wrong reasons. It should not matter how much you spend or where you get married or who is there. What matters is the love that you both have for each other and the commitment you have just agreed to.

Donna R. wrote: Screw all that nonsense; just elope and send everyone an e-mail telling them you are married! lol

Sheila wrote: I used to plan weddings and I always advised brides they had to live after the wedding. I had one client who came in and gave me the final payment of $10,000 in cash. Besides the fact I had to count a bunch of 10s, 20s and 50-dollar bills, the bride called me a year later and told me they divorced.

■ ■ ■

The point that Sheila made about the couples divorcing within a year of the wedding happens more often than you think. The couple barely return home from the honeymoon, and they're filing for a divorce or annulment. Once all the magic and attention goes away, sometimes so does the interest in being married.

This is precisely why I wrote this chapter. Couples must stop getting carried away with the extravagant weddings at the expense of their financial security. The only people who matter on your wedding day are you and your spouse; that's it! If couples are smart, they will invest their hard-earned money into a college fund, pay down their debt or put a down payment on a first home. I know that doesn't sound sexy, but having debt will suck the passion out of your marriage faster than the last cold beer at a family reunion!

111

I know this may sound redundant but I have to reiterate. A marriage is lifetime responsibility not a staged event that ends after the reception. We want the ring but not the responsibility. We want the ceremony but not the commitment. We want the richer but not the poorer, the thick but not the thin. But marriage isn't a buffet where you can pick and choose which vows you want to submit to. And simply calling yourself husband and wife doesn't make your problems disappear. As soon as the ceremony is over, nothing magical is going to happen. You're going to be the same two people with the same unresolved issues when the lights go out! And an expensive ring and flashy ceremony won't change that!

Would You Sign
A Prenuptial Agreement?

If you really want to find out what kind of person you're about to marry, bring up the topic of prenuptial agreements. There's nothing that unmasks a person's greed, insecurities and selfishness like the topic of money! Some believe that asking your partner to sign a prenuptial is a sign of distrust and a lack of faith in the marriage; others feel it is the person who refuses to sign who is guilty of wanting to take advantage in the event that the marriage fails.

When I discussed this topic with men and women online, it started a heated debate. For the most part, men were for prenuptials and women were against them. However, the women who were "Pro-Prenuptial" had two things in common: They were either financially well-off or they had gone through a hellish divorce. What follows are some of the comments and interviews. Take notes because there were valid points made on both sides of the issue.

Jacque wrote: I totally agree! And whoever doesn't want to protect themselves from vultures must want to be eaten alive.

Sydney wrote: I don't have much but I do have a house, and when I got married (divorced a year later), my husband was more than happy to sign one to make sure my house went to my kids. I had the house years before I met him!!

Cbonita wrote: If you are marrying for the right reasons, you would not need a prenuptial contract. Unfortunately, oftentimes when things go sour in the relationship, you see a different person. So if you have wealth and the other person does not, do what you need to do to protect yourself.

James wrote: Women are the first ones in a relationship who see the picture from only one side — theirs! When it comes to a prenup, all they see are dollar signs and getting cut out of something. If they were the ones with something to lose instead of something to gain, that picture would be in full view.

Charles wrote: All of y'all talk that bull crap. After a marriage is over, females want to destroy a man or vice versa. If you have something to protect and you don't get a prenup signed, that's just stupid. Some states have laws anyway to protect women, giving them half a man's retirement, but damn, don't let her walk away with your house and Mercedes, too. lol

Doris wrote: Hmmm, I say sign it! People change and become greedy. Love walks out, and so does everything you worked your whole life for. No matter what goes wrong, be it infidelity or neglect, no one deserves to walk out the door with your life's work, or even half of it. Protect yourself, people; relationships aren't perfect; neither are the people in them.

Tina wrote: I agree 100%!!! FYI: People have been known to do some scandalous things in the midst of a divorce! So I say better safe than sorry!

Ayne wrote: There is nothing wrong with this agreement. In fact, if you don't have one, then you are not very smart. It's about mutual disclosure. There are things I have achieved and want to protect, and my spouse has attained certain things he wants to protect, but we also have made provisions for one another and our children. Everything we amass together will be equally divided, but all things prior to our union are protected. I love him more than the world; it's 24 yrs later. Sign it and get on with your marriage!

Aminah wrote: I don't know why people think marriages aren't business relationships also, which are solely based on the laws surrounding marriage and dissolution thereof. You are essentially entering a business agreement under the law! Why pretend that doesn't exist? Be in love but don't stick your head in the sand.

Michelle C. wrote: I was against a prenup until I found myself faced with having to give my ex-husband half of my hard-earned pension. Imagine after raising two kids with no child support, then being faced with having to give a man half of your retirement income every month. Thank goodness for my very capable lawyer. Yes, Michael, we want a prenup; we want a prenup!!!! lmbo

Rachelle wrote: I see both sides. People who really love each other don't start a marriage thinking theirs will end, regardless of the statistics. The prenup could make one person feel the other doesn't love them enough. On the other hand, marriage is a contractual agreement, an investment like any other & should be treated that way as well. That wisdom can build fruitful marriages. That investment should be weighed & considered among the others with both parties' risk/loss factors in mind and both parties' value systems. If my partner had more financial stability than I did, but I gave up one life for a life with that person anticipating this will be my lifestyle going forward, and this was promised till death do us part, not divorce — I would require an allotment for that in the prenup that doesn't entitle me to the family home. Which by the way if it's "your" family home, then don't move me in it because then it becomes my home, too. Basically I'm all about prenuptial agreements as long as they're mutually beneficial. Marriage is a contractual agreement & should not be taken lightly spiritually, emotionally or financially. All you bitter people out there, stay single.

■ ■ ■

We must stop being afraid to have difficult conversations about prenuptial and other issues related to money. We treat it like sex education with our children, in that we believe that if we talk about sex it will make them want to go out and do it, but actually the reverse is true. Education is prevention, and although ignorance may be bliss, it costs, big time! Talking about prenuptials is no different. It's an opportunity to discuss financial issues, debt, paying bills and other issues that contribute to the No. 1 cause of divorce. It can also reveal some of our partner's insecurities about marriage, as well as our own.

The topic of prenuptial agreements should not be seen as an opportunity for one person to take advantage of the other but instead as a chance to find out what your partner's expectations are in the event things don't work out. If you're the person coming to the table with less, then use this topic as an opportunity to find out how much or how little your partner values you. On the other hand, if you're the partner who has the majority of the assets, then why not find out in advance if your partner is marrying you for love or for your money? Either way, you'll learn something about your partner that you didn't know, which could help in making a decision about whether to move forward with the marriage or not. Even if you only have a small pension and live in a one-bedroom apartment, the topic of prenuptials is relevant. Remember, it's not about the amount of wealth you have but what you both see as fair. That's something I would want to know if I were getting married. Wouldn't you?

But no matter which side of the table you're on, don't you dare consider signing a contract of marriage without first hashing out your money issues! It can destroy a marriage faster than any affair. The partner with the least should be realistic about what he or she should expect and will be entitled to. After all, he or she is investing in the relationship, too. And if you're the one with the most to lose financially, don't be a fool and be blinded by love. Treat your partner with respect and fairness, but always protect your own interests.

■ ■ ■

It's sad that with all the information and statistics about failed marriages on the Internet, in magazine articles and on TV talk shows, most people continue to be blinded by the romantic fantasies of marriage and love. No matter what the record shows, there are those who will always feel that there's no place for business in a marriage. Here's a comment by a woman on my web page that makes my point. I felt compelled to respond to her.

Christine wrote: No I wouldn't sign a prenup because it's a form of control and power. And where is God in all of this?

My response: Christine, if there is NO prenuptial, doesn't the person who has less wealth now have all the power? And prenups can be written to make sure your partner is taken care of in the event that the marriage fails, which half of them do. And what if your parents left you a home that has been in your family for generations? Wouldn't you want to protect that? And what about a business you built that you want to leave your children? That's not worth protecting?

If you build something together, then you should share in it 50-50, but if that man or woman built it before you entered their lives, why wouldn't you agree not to be entitled to that income, business or investment? Maybe it's the person who won't sign who has the trust issues.

And regarding your question about God, people going on about how God and faith should be at the foundation of a marriage are missing one point; the foundation has to be built on communication and trust. The presence of God can't be separated from the principles of God, and trust and honest communication should be at the top of the list. But if you insist on taking the business out of marriage, then why not just be married in your hearts with God's blessing. That's what marriage really is anyway. But once you entered into a contract of marriage, it became a business whether you like it or not and, therefore, should be treated accordingly. You can't have it both ways.

■ ■ ■

Christine's point is typical of how we have completely romanticized marriage without any regard for the realities of day-to-day life as a married couple. Money is central to most relationships, whether it's paying bills, buying a house, having good credit, investing for retirement, saving for college, etc. We must stop living in this fantasy world that tells us relationships are all about falling in love and holding hands skipping through the park; marriages are businesses, too. Anyone who doesn't understand that is in for a rude awakening. It's a contract of marriage, people!!!

That's why it's best to sit down and talk about what's fair while everyone is thinking rationally because once you get involved in divorce proceedings, you'll see a side of your partner that will completely shock you. The person you once vowed "Till death do us part" will be fighting you to the death over a toaster oven, blender, even an artificial plant just to get revenge!

When Someone Shows You Who They Are, Believe Them

When your fiancé cheated on you before the wedding, not once but twice, did you think that getting married would transform him into being faithful? When she withdrew money from the joint bank account without your permission to buy shoes and expensive clothes, why did you believe she would change just because you gave her the label of wife? And when you were verbally and physically abused, did you really believe that you could love the abuse out of him or her after the wedding?

Listen, folks, having a wedding ceremony won't change your partner into a better person or into someone else! This idea that reciting vows in front of your family, friends and in the presence of God Almighty will make your relationship better is nothing but a fantasy. If he or she was annoying, disrespectful, abusive, dishonest and irresponsible before the wedding, they'll be annoying, disrespectful, abusive, dishonest and irresponsible after the wedding. What you see is what you get!

How many of you remember the old newspaper cartoon called "Love Is"? Each day there was a different expression of the word love. For example, Love is … never having to say I'm sorry! Or Love is … taking one day at a time. Get it? But the one "Love Is" cartoon that everyone needs to read is, Love is … acceptance. If you're seriously considering getting married or being in a committed relationship, you'd better cut and paste this on your wall. If you don't accept a person for who they are, then that's not love, that's delusion! And so is the idea that loving someone hard enough will change them!

But the truth is you can't change people just by loving them. Love may be a powerful thing but it's not magic! You can't just wave your overwhelming love over someone's head, and they miraculously change into Mr. or Mrs. Right. There is no amount of love on earth that can change a person who doesn't want to change. But hold that thought; I'll come back to it.

Let's address this issue of why people are trying to change their partners in the first place. I thought the whole idea of getting married was to love the person for who they are, not for who you want them to be or for the person they have the potential to be. If the idea is to make a lifetime commitment, doesn't it make sense to be with someone you're already happy and satisfied with? And besides, who has the energy to make over a grown man or woman? Just the thought of it is exhausting. I've got a better idea — why not choose a person who's already good enough for you.

But that's obviously too much work, or should I say, it takes too much time. We want love now, happiness now, marriage now. So what if the guy has some anger issues, or if the woman is disrespectful at times? Some people believe that once they slip that ring on his or her finger, all their problems will magically disappear. Who needs a mate that's perfect for them? When you're desperate to be married, many people will settle for a project instead of a partner. In their minds if they could just fix one, or two, or maybe three things, that person would make the perfect half of a super couple. I call it the "Fix-A-Dude" or "Fix-A-Chick" syndrome.

But these Makeover Marriages never work out because no matter how much surgery you pay for, no matter how much you try to dress them up or teach them which fork is for the salad, you can't make someone into something they're not and, most importantly, into someone they don't want to be. As the saying goes, class cannot be bought; you can't turn a ho into a housewife or househusband, and love does not conquer all!

We throw around the word "Love" too easily, and we give our love away too freely. People are so desperate to be happy that they are quick to jump at the word love, the emotions of love, the magic of love, just for the sake of escaping being alone!

We want to be happy now! And what's the fastest and easiest way to find happiness, to fall in love, or to believe in love at first sight? We crave love because it gives us a high, like a drug … it's a quick fix! We are programmed by Hollywood to be swept off our feet and live happily every after.

Well, I hate to burst your bubble, but that's not reality. Reality is waking up every day, paying bills, getting the kids off to school, doing homework, making mistakes, getting on each other's nerves, compromising, fighting, making up, and getting up the next day and starting all over again. And you do it with a person you love for who they are, not for what you secretly desire them to be. That's what a real relationship is about. That doesn't sound sexy, does it? And it sure as hell doesn't sound easy!

But what do I know? I'm just a man with an opinion, right? Well, I'll tell you what I do know. I've been on this planet for over 50 years; that's a long time if you're constantly growing and learning. I was also married once; not many people know that about me. We met while I was in the Air Force stationed at Scott AFB in Illinois. She was a beautiful Southern girl from Alabama who taught me a lot about compromise, patience and commitment.

I've also had many other relationships, both long and short term, and I learned a lot from those experiences, too, like being honest from day one, the importance of being consistent, and to accept a woman for who she is and not try to mold her into my ideal. But like most of life's most valuable lessons, you don't learn to apply them until after the relationship is over and someone has been hurt. So it only makes sense that those of us who have already been down this road should warn those behind us so they don't drive off the same cliff. We may not be able to save everyone, but at least we can reduce the number of fatalities.

We must all agree, starting today, to stop feeding the younger generation this "Cinderella and Prince Charming" fairytale that tells that love trumps respect, common values, responsibility, honesty, integrity, consistency, temperament, chemistry, and, the one we don't hear often enough, compatibility. Love can be a wonderful thing when it's put in its proper place. It's the foundation of a marriage, but without those other elements, it's just a foundation with no roof or plumbing.

Relationships are work. Strong relationships take time to build. Relationships are about being real about who you are and being happy with who your partner is as a person without conditions. And in relationships, you don't always get your way; it's called compromise, and it ain't easy!

But I promise you this, if you go into it with your eyes open and remove the rose-colored glasses, you'll have a much better chance at "happily every after" or, at the very least, "peacefully ever after," and what's more valuable than that?

■ ■ ■

A close friend of mine was at the Essence Music Festival in New Orleans having a conversation with a group of married men and women, and my name came up. None of them was aware that the gentleman and I knew each other. As the conversation went on, one of the women blurted out, "I don't like Michael Baisden; he's anti-marriage." My friend immediately pulled out his phone and dialed my number, but he didn't tell them whom he was calling. He sat the phone down and let me listen in to the conversation. Boy, did I get an earful! Now before I tell you what was said, I have to admit that I understand how someone could have that perception of me. First of all, I do speak mostly about issues related to single people. I am single, and single people in my opinion have more issues, such as how to not be single. Having said that, let's get back to this conversation.

After listening in to some of the fair and unfair character-izations of my radio show and me personally, my buddy told them who was on the phone. Of course, the most vocal woman got quiet; meanwhile, everybody else started cracking up. Hell, I was laughing, too. Once she finally agreed to talk to me, my friend put me on speakerphone, and this is what I told her.

"Ma'am, I am not anti-marriage, but I am anti-bad marriage. There's nothing more fulfilling than a good marriage, and a bad marriage is a living hell! I respect people who are happily married, but I don't respect marriage just because people say they are married or have been married a long time. It's about the quality of time you spend in a relationship, not the quantity. And yes, I am speaking from experience. Before I let you go, congratulations on your marriage; I'm sure you and your husband are very happy."

Her husband must have been listening because I heard a man clear his throat very loud! Umh Umm! The next thing I heard was a loud smack, and then an eruption of laughter. She must have smacked the snot outta him. But the point I was trying to make was that too often people go into marriage believing it's going to change things, fix what's broken and wash away all of your sins. But what really happens is that getting married only magnifies all of your unresolved issues.

During one of my shows on marriage, I posted a comment asking my listeners to share their views. I called it "Finish This Sentence." This is what I posted: "Please Finish This Sentence. The reason why my marriage failed is because (blank)." The letter you're about to read was inspired by the response e-mailed by Glenn from Los Angeles.

Glenn wrote: The reason why my marriage failed is because I was too in love with my life to see that we were not compatible in the bedroom or when it came to communicating. We met back in college and reunited in our early 30s. Everyone just assumed we would eventually get married. It's amazing how other people's expectations can make you feel pressured to do something that deep down inside you know is a bad decision. I proposed to my wife back in 2008. She was

35, I was 38. I figured at that age I was old enough to handle the responsibility of a wife and family. But being responsible is not enough to guarantee a successful marriage; neither is commitment or compromise. None of those things matter if you're not honest with yourself about who you are and who your partner is before you get married. It's a shame that I didn't realize that until after my divorce was final. As you mature, you learn valuable lessons about relationships, such as how falling in love can blind you to who your partner truly is, and it can make you delusional about your own limitations.

I thought my love was so strong that it would take away my desire for other women, and it did for six months or so, but once the newness of being married wore off, I was out in the streets trying to compensate for what I wasn't getting at home. It began with casual flirting, then texting, Facebook, tweets and then full-blown affairs.

I learned the hard way that falling in love doesn't change your values, your morals, your temperament, and it damn sure won't improve your sex life. I loved my wife; I loved her so much I ignored the fact that we weren't sexually compatible and that she was combative about everything! I don't know how I missed that! It got so bad she would damn near start a debate about whether the sky was blue. It was that serious. I knew she had abandonment issues with her father but like an idiot I married her anyway. I figured the minute I slipped that 5-carat diamond ring on her finger that she would instantly respect me as a man and her husband and get buck-naked and start swinging off the chandelier. But a year into the marriage she still was argumentative and stiff as a board in bed. I had so many nights when I would go into the bathroom after sex and look at my reflection in the mirror. There I was, damn near 40 years old, and I was having the worst sex of my life. I felt tricked and trapped.

I hope that every man who is considering getting married will listen to my story and take notes. Giving a woman the label of wife and putting that so-called "Magic Ring" on her finger won't change a damn thing. The combative, close-minded and sexually incompatible person you're engaged to will be the same combative, close-minded and sexually incompatible person you get after you say "I do!"

Ab-ra-ca-dab-ra ... ho-cus-po-cus ... and ... poof! Next thing you know, you're married to your future ex!

Whatever Works

You can always pick the couples that are happily married out of the crowd. They're usually the ones all hugged up like they're on a first date; they smile and laugh as they wait on their table at a restaurant, or sometimes they walk quietly through the park holding hands enjoying each other's company. Happily married couples finish each other's sentences, she wipes the sloppy food from the corner of his mouth, and he's constantly kissing and groping her in public. They're so in love they almost make you sick to watch. I'm joking but you get the point.

"What's their secret?" you ask. It's simple. They chose partners they were compatible with; they were ready to be in a committed relationship; they took lessons from other successful couples; they didn't waste time with people who didn't want to be married; most importantly, they set up their own rules and boundaries. And that's precisely what every married couple has to do if they want to have longevity; they must customize their relationship in a way that works best for them.

Too often people make the mistake of trying to be married the way their friends are married, or the way their parents were married, or how they see marriage played out on television. But you're not your friends or parents, and your marriage is not a scripted TV show; it's real, and it's unique! The reason why there's no universal template for how to be married or how to be a normal husband or normal wife is because there's no such thing as a normal marriage!

Couples are stepping outside the box to create marriages that work for them. For some people that means writing their own vows. I know that may sound like blasphemy to some, but why should couples be limited to a cookie-cutter script instead of writing their own promises and declarations to the person they love that speaks from their heart and not just out of tradition? Besides, not all tradition is good or practical. I know plenty of intelligent and forward-thinking women who have issues with the traditional vows that read "love, honor and obey." The love and honor part is fine, but OBEY? What is this, the Stone Age? How about replacing the word obey with respect? And while you're at it, throw in, "I promise not to buy a ton of shoes; I promise to save my husband some closet space, and I promise to keep my girlfriends and family out of our business!" Now those are the kind of promises a husband needs his wife to make before God! But to obey? Give me a break!

And let's not forget the verse in the vows that reads, "Until death do us part." Now how many billions of people have gotten divorced and broken that vow? How about rewriting it to read, "As long as we love and cherish each other." Isn't that more practical? When I posted this topic of customizing wedding vows on my web page the responses were interesting and entertaining.

> **Jessica wrote:** In a marriage the word obey actually means to obey God first! But men think it means they can boss a woman around like a slave. So until men become better leaders and less controlling, I say get rid of it, delete it, use white out if necessary!

> **Christina wrote:** The love and honor is not outdated at all. And, yes, couples should make up their own vows if that's what they want to do. But that obey part is definitely a hell-to-the-No!

> **DeAnna wrote:** It depends on the couple. Some couples should NOT write their own vows. Have you heard the way some people talk? lol

Amela wrote: Obey should be taken out of the vows because it gives the man a sense of being the ole mighty ruler of the woman, and it's not so. It's an equal partnership! Aretha Franklin said it best; it's not about obeying, it's about R-E-S-P-E-C-T.

Judy wrote: I would NEVER vow to not take up all the closet space. It would be just too hard to keep that one, so why lie? lol

■ ■ ■

Another tradition of marriage that is changing is the ritual of exchanging wedding bands. Some couples have decided not to symbolize their marriage with a piece of metal. I personally don't have an issue with wedding bands, but I can understand how the focus on rings or jewelry can often place more emphasis on the symbols of marriage rather than the examples of marriage. Besides, most people don't care if you're wearing a wedding ring or not, they're going to approach you anyway! It's a man's or woman's demeanor and confidence in their marriage that sends the strongest message, not a piece of jewelry. But that's just my opinion. When I posted this topic about wedding bands online, passions got high on both sides.

Darren wrote: Where in the Bible does it say, thou shall buy diamond rings and gold bands to symbolize your love for each other? That's some man-made bull crap to make money and to brand people!

Diana wrote: Too many people think that a ring makes them married. Well it doesn't; just like taking it off doesn't make you unmarried. Some people probably wouldn't even get married without a ring, as if the ring means more than the commitment itself.

Deborah wrote: It's a piece of jewelry. Nothing more. The bond a married couple has are the vows you made before God. It's not about the ring on the finger. That's just to show to outside people you are married. If you love your spouse and respect your vows, then a piece of jewelry means nothing!

Nikkie wrote: If he doesn't wear his ring, I will tattoo my name on his forehead lmao

Dawn wrote: Wow, it's sad to hear a ring symbolizes commitment; you mean the significant other's word is not enough? My grandparents didn't wear rings, but their commitment to each other was very evident — 50+ yrs together till death did they part. Guess it's the change of time, cause nowadays a ring doesn't ward off anyone. Some look specifically for men with a ring.

Eric wrote: Doesn't matter if you wear it or not, what kind, or how much the ring costs. Bottom line is the commitment to your spouse in your heart, because in the beginning there was no ring but the commitment was still there.

Meshell wrote: I believe that entirely too much emphasis and importance is placed on a man-made piece of metal that is placed on the third finger of your left hand, as well as weddings themselves. Marriage does not consist of a "ring and a date." If you believe that you didn't get married until you stood before a minister or judge, and he pronounced you man and wife, your relationship may be in serious trouble.

Marriage begins in the heart, mind and spirit when two people decide to devote and dedicate themselves to each other. Marriage has nothing to do with a ring and a date. Marriage between two people is something that is nurtured and cultivated over a period of time. I could care less whether or not someone wore their wedding ring. It's a superficial piece of jewelry, which, in the larger scheme of things, means absolutely nothing! A ring never stopped a married person from cheating if that's what they wanted to do, and quite frankly most people today have no respect for what a ring was designed for. It is supposed to be a symbol to the world that an individual has devoted themselves to one person. Now it can mean anything from "yes, I'm married and proud of it" to "come check me out ... I'm married so we can hook up with no strings attached."

You have to figure out for yourself where your priority lies. Does it lie in the man/woman that wears their rings religiously but always seems to find ways and reasons to lie and disrespect their marriage, or does it lie in the heart of the man/woman that rarely and/or never wears their rings, but puts their marriage only second to God? Your choice... IJS

Carliss wrote: I find it so interesting: Men have a fit when their spouse does not wear her ring, yet it's okay for them NOT to wear their wedding ring. I know when I get married, I'm getting my husband's wedding band a half size too small so he CAN'T take it off. I just want the ladies to know, HE'S MINE, BACK OFF!!!!!

■ ■ ■

The reasons why people want their partners to wear a wedding band range from respect for long-standing traditions to a blatant act to brand their partners for the world to see. But no matter what their motivation, it boils down to whatever works for that couple. No matter what my opinion is, or that of friends and family, it's *your* marriage! Or as the Isley Brothers song goes, "It's your thang, do what you wanna do, I can't tell ya, who to sock it to."

Customizing a marriage or relationship also means setting your own rules about what is allowed and what is out of bounds. For example, a woman's married girlfriend may insist that her husband be home by midnight, whereas you're okay with your husband coming home any time before the sun comes up. Likewise, a man may be okay with his wife taking a vacation out of the country without him, but his buddy wouldn't even consider allowing his wife to travel without him.

The most challenging part about having these rules between you and your partner is that it doesn't require anyone else's approval; however, those outside of the relationship are observing and making judgments. This is where the couple has to draw the line. The first time anyone makes a comment that is contrary to what the couple has agreed on, they must be put in check immediately and firmly! If you don't make it clear that your marriage rules are not open for discussion, your friends, family and co-workers will constantly interject their opinions and values on your relationship. That's a recipe for disaster!

Many couples have ended close friendships simply because the friends could not accept how the other couple was conducting their marriage. The reason why this usually happens is because the couple that is living the more restrictive marriage is threatened by the openness and security of the couple that is allowing more freedom. The last thing they want is for their partner to start getting ideas. Some people are okay with their husband or wife having sex outside the marriage; it can be an open understanding or unspoken, but it is allowed. That may annoy or even anger those outside of the relationship, but it's not for them to judge. If it works for that couple, in the end that's all that matters.

My advice to couples who want to be in a happy, long-term marriage is to use the examples of healthy marriages around you, set your own rules, establish your own boundaries, and tell everyone else to mind their own damn business!

Marriages change because the people in them change. It's called maturing, evolving ... growing up. But the real question is, why would you expect them not to change? Getting together with a compatible person can be a challenge, but it's growing together that takes the most work!

~ Michael Baisden

I'm Not The Same
Person You Married

The person you married 5, 10, 15 or 20 years ago is not the same person you're lying next to in bed today. And the younger you are when you get married, the truer this statement is. Some couples are able to make the adjustment as they go through their life journey together, while others grow apart and become yet another statistic. I've always wondered why this aspect of marriage is so rarely, if ever, discussed. The emphasis is always on love, communication, honesty, compromise and respect, which are all important, but the issue of change is just as crucial. When we enter into marriage, one thing should be made crystal clear to the bride and groom from day one: Change is coming.

Change is constant, whether it's our children growing up, changing careers, or the change we experience within ourselves over the years. We're constantly going through different phases in our lives. But imagine going through those phases with another person who is also growing and changing at the same time, but not necessarily at the same rate. Now add to that equation that all of this change is happening while living under the same roof and sleeping in the same bed. Now that's what I call a challenge!

Who you are today will not be the person you evolve into tomorrow, not mentally, emotionally, physically, occupationally, spiritually, temperamentally, and not sexually. Even our taste in food changes. And if you're not going through changes, something is wrong; either that or you're dead! Change is happening every day whether you acknowledge it or not.

But the question is not whether we change, the real dilemma for couples is can they change and grow together? When you committed to spending the rest of your lives together, no one ever said, "Oh, by the way, your partner is going to be different a few years from now, so be ready to adjust." The reality is someone who may seem perfect for you today could be a disaster tomorrow. Sure, growing together is possible but only if we keep the lines of communication open and we don't lose our individuality just because we're married.

Delores wrote: I once read a joke that said love is blind and marriage is a real eye-opener. Man, ain't that the truth? When you're young and full of love and optimism, you don't think about what this person you're marrying will be like ten or fifteen years into the future. You dive in with no idea of who you are or who your partner is; that's hard to know at 21. And many years into the marriage you look up and both of you are completely different people than you were when you got married. That's what happened in my marriage. When we celebrated our fourteen-year anniversary, we had to sit down and re-evaluate our entire relationship. Since our daughter was entering high school, we had more time to focus on our relationship, which can be a scary thing to do after you've been focusing on work and your child all those years. I've seen marriages completely fall apart after the children become more independent, or after they leave home for college. They look at each other and ask, "So, tell me, why are we still together?"

Fortunately, my husband and I still enjoy each other's company and the passion is still there. But we are nowhere near the same two people who met fifteen years ago. The challenge is to ask yourself, Do I still love this person? And are we still growing together? If the answer is no, don't wait, get out! I've seen way too many couples who are just a marriage on paper and it's a sad thing to watch.

Lelia wrote: I don't think the person changes, I think they just show you who they really are. Sometimes people will try to be what they think you want them to be just to get you. That's what I went through in my previous marriage. That's why I had to throw that small fish back and keep fishing until I found a bigger and better fish. If you get an honest man or woman, they won't change because you will see the real person when you are dating. If you don't like what you see, then don't marry them. Now, the first couple of years is an adjustment period because you are blending two different people together. You have to learn to adjust and compromise with each other and after some time this should work itself out. You have to communicate and respect each other. Each year it should get better. I've been with my husband for 16 years and each year is different and better. If you're with someone and it's getting worse each year, then perhaps that's not your soul mate and you may need to bounce!!! But bottom line is, people don't change, only the circumstances do. That's my opinion.

Robin wrote: We all evolve, it's not just your mate who's evolving, and you will both make mistakes; no-body's perfect. During the "dry" seasons, you have to think the best of each other and not the worst. You have to keep laughter in your marriage and above all have God in your lives. Lastly, a lot of changes happen prior to marriage, watch out for the red flags! They're waving at you for a reason! Change is one thing but Dr. Jekyll turning into Mr. Hyde is something else entirely.

Shermell wrote: Change will come. I've been with my husband for 17 years and most definitely we've both changed. But unlike other couples we choose to change together. Yes, we are both two different people, but we love each other too much to allow anything or anybody to separate us. We talk to each other, not at each other; we take into consideration how the other feels (this means that it's not all about you), we listen even if the one who is talking is wrong; we communicate (openly); we compromise (a lot) but we do it. Now I'm not saying that everything is all peaches and cream and that we don't as they say "get in our feelings." We just know that divorce is not an option in our marriage. What you did to get that person is the same thing you have to do to keep them. I don't care how much change you go though, you have to make your marriage a priority.

Ife wrote: Change is life's only constant; we live, we grow, we evolve. At the same time, the core of who we are is developed early on in life, and that is something that doesn't usually change. Becoming someone you don't recognize ... someone in stark contrast to the person you married ... that's usually not "becoming," but more like an "unveiling." To me that says a person wasn't being authentic from the start. That's something very different. But the natural things that may change about us over time, whether through life experiences, just getting older, etc., these are things we have to learn to accept if we truly love our spouses and want our marriages to sustain the test of time. Be patient and understanding; be committed and communicate. If you truly love and respect one another, you can find middle ground no matter how much change you go through. Too many people use "Change" as an excuse to act as a fool in the relationship. If that's the case, you need to help them "change" their address.

■ ■ ■

I'm constantly encouraging my readers to have a vision for their lives. And that includes having a vision for their relationships. When you visualize your ideal future, you're challenged to move beyond the emotional aspects of the relationship. How you feel is a given, you love your partner. Okay, but what's next? Visualization changes the focus from love to destination. Where are we going? How do we get there? And is this the person going to make that future more or less possible?

I know this can seem complicated but it really isn't. If we simply pay more attention to the mentality, work ethic and values of our partners we could make better decisions for our future. For example, if you envision starting your own business but you know your partner is not a risk taker, that man or woman may not be a person you can get to the next level with. If you desire to live in a diverse part of the country or the world but your partner is homophobic and racist, that future is probably not going to materialize. My point is, having a vision for your future allows you to make better relationship choices in your present. The ideal of marriage is to stay together, FOREVER! So it stands to reason that you need a person that is not only compatible for the present but for the rest of your life. And there's one thing that will kill that in a hot second: choosing a partner who is close-minded!

As I stated before, people do change and along with it so do their appetites. I used to hate red wines; now I can barely tolerate whites. Back in my 20s and 30s I couldn't stand tomatoes and mushrooms, but now I try to eat them with nearly every meal. And as for sex, well, let me just say I've always been the adventurous type. There's nothing I won't try at least once. Okay, maybe there are one or two things I wouldn't try, but you get the idea. And I would never date a woman who didn't have the same open attitude about sex. That's what being sexually compatible is all about.

The challenge, however, is navigating those changing appetites with the person you met 5, 10, 15 or 20-plus years ago. Although your sexual desires and curiosities may have peaked, your partner may be perfectly satisfied with missionary-position sex in the bedroom with all the lights out. And because we know our partners better than they know themselves, one of the partners has already made the decision not to even suggest trying something new. They already know from living with their partner that his or her fantasy about threesomes, anal sex or going to a swingers club is not going to happen. Some people aren't open for trying chocolate ice cream instead of vanilla. Being close-minded sexually is a one-way ticket to infidelity and/or divorce court.

But in the spirit of trying to keep the passion alive in our marriages, I asked some of my friends who have been married for five or more years for advice on how they kept the fire burning. You might want to write a few of these ideas down. I know I did.

Rosco J. wrote: It's been 15 years and we're still going strong! People think it's rocket science keeping a marriage together for this long, but to me it's simple. I have my own life and so does my wife. She takes a vacation alone every year and so do I, and we take one together. We have friends in common and we have our own. She has a room in the house with her personal things and I have my toys in the garage. People who get married better understand one important thing going into it; you have to allow your partner to have their own identity. It's no different than when you were dating; that's what made it so exciting. You had your own places, then you would get together and do things. My wife and I still date. And when that starts to get boring, we throw a little twist in there, like role-playing. Women are not the only ones who need to strip for their partners. My wife is very sexual and I know I have to keep in shape just to keep up. It's like she hit another gear when she turned 50. I was like, what did you do with my wife? lol

Jamie F. wrote: It's not just women who change, men do, too. My husband went from being this conservative church boy at 21 to hosting swingers parties by the time we were in our mid-30s. At first, I was ready to leave the marriage, mainly because I felt that he was compensating for what I was lacking, but we sat down and had a heart-to-heart talk, and he explained to me that this was his way of making our marriage last. At first I thought that was a bunch of crap, but to this day I have no reason to believe he ever cheated on me. His attitude was, whatever we do, we will do it together. At first I was reluctant, but after I allowed myself to really get to know the other couples, I relaxed and was able to be in that open environment without feeling threatened.

My first time swinging with another couple was not as difficult as I thought it would be, especially with my husband right there beside me. He was clear that if I didn't like it, we would stop and he would never ask me to try it again. Now, I'm the one sending out invitations and hosting parties. It's like a complete metamorphosis.

Ladies, I'm not trying to sell you on this lifestyle, it is not for everyone. The point is to be open to trying new things. Too often we get caught up in guilt and worrying about what other people will think instead of focusing on our partner and the marriage. If the idea is to be together until death do us part, you might have to step outside your comfort zone. Forever can be a long time if you're not willing to take some risks. I trusted my husband and now I have a life I never could have imagined. I hate to think of what things would be like had I just run away instead of having an open mind. I guess it boils down to how much you love your partner and how much you trust him.

Felecia S. wrote: I can't even talk to my girlfriends about sex. They are so holier than thou it's impossible to make them understand the changes that both men and women go through in the course of a marriage, especially if they are both very sexual. My husband and I have raised three beautiful kids, gotten them all off to college, and we're still crazy about each other after 25 years. We went through a lot of the usual ups and downs, and yes, we both have changed. We met in college at 19 years old and now we're in our early 40s. Of course, there's a difference. However, instead of fighting it, like my girlfriends, we embraced it.

Over time our diets have changed, our bodies have changed, and our attitudes about sex have changed. You know, when you have a house full of kids, there's not a lot of time for spontaneous sex. My husband used to call it red light, green light sex, like the game. We had to get it in quick before one of the kids knocked on the door. But now that they're gone, honey, let me tell you, we are knocking holes in the walls. Thank God we live in a house because if we were in an apartment, we would have been evicted a long time ago. lol

I can share everything with my husband; that's something else that we've gotten better with over time. When we were younger, I think we were too afraid of hurting the other person's feelings, but after 40 it was like we both said, what the hell! And all those things started to come out that we never discussed. Again, I think having the kids out opened up an opportunity to create an entirely new relationship and it's exciting. I have the man I love, whom I know, and who knows me, after 25 years in my life sharing new things. It's unreal! And what I enjoy most is being able to share my sexual fantasies. Even though I probably won't do half of the stuff we talk about, just saying it takes our sex to new heights. My poor girlfriends don't even watch pornography with their husbands. Booor–ring! My husband and I are so regular at the strip clubs they have a table reserved for us. And I get more lap dances than he does. lol

Dayna wrote: I'm gonna jump in as one of the younger posters on here. For all you ladies that are saying, "keep it simple," just remember that younger women don't mind trying out new things. So you better start opening yourselves up to truth, trust and intimacy with your mate. We aren't our grandmas. Get comfortable in your bodies and handle your business before someone else does.

Paula wrote: Out of the bag of tricks: get a black cat suit, some stilettos, a SWAT cap and a water gun. Fill the water gun with flavored massage oil. "Arrest" him, do a strip search, shoot the massage oil and go ham. We like to have fun. Your idea of fun may be different but that works for us. Role playing, spontaneity and laughter!

Shauna wrote: My ex-husband was extremely close-minded. He told me after we got married that he had bedded over 100 women, and I realized why nobody was coming back for seconds. He wasn't eating the peaches but always had his legs open and ready for me to step up to the mic. Don't get me wrong. I continued to do it because it gave me pleasure to do, but I grew tired of the madness. I like it strong and long and he was not cutting it. Communication stopped because he was offended that I wanted to discuss ways to improve our lackluster sex life. How can you be in denial? Had it ever dawned on him that most women, especially this one, will never be ok with a five-minute man. It's important to find someone that is compatible with you in the bedroom. If you are not adventurous and have no desire to do things that push the envelope, please pass me by because truth be told, we can have the best situation financially, but if you can't put me to sleep on a regular basis, it won't work. Check back with me in 20 years, it just might be enough but not now sweetie. I like making the walls sweat and I'd rather it be the ones in my home with my spouse because I would love to be married again, but this time with someone who can appreciate that I might look like a good girl in public but will blow your mind behind closed doors in every room of the house.

Tekesha wrote: My guy and I would turn our room into a dungeon, have the lights off with candles everywhere, and the door to our room would be wide open that led to the outside patio. We like to record ourselves, so we turn on the camera and role-play. I would be his sex slave chained in handcuffs letting him dominate me, then we would switch the story board around and have intercourse completely nude outside in the pouring rain on the patio. Did we start out like this in our marriage? Of course not, but thank goodness we grew in our desires together. I have girlfriends and co-workers who secretly want to express themselves sexually in the same way, but their husbands have grown so accustomed to the same boring sex for 15-plus years they don't dare reveal themselves. So they have to live vicariously through me, and I have all the toys and videos to send them over the edge. I feel sorry for them, but that's what happens when you and your partner don't grow together!

■ ■ ■

There's nothing more painful than realizing the person you love, raised children with and have invested 10 or more years of your life with won't change or can't change. I know people who won't even try a different dish at a restaurant; they literally order the same thing off the menu for years. It's hard to accept that you and your partner are growing apart. It happens every day. One person wants to further their education and move to another city; the other person is satisfied with their 9-to-5 and doesn't want to move away from their family. Or one partner wants to explore different sexual appetites, but his or her spouse is comfortable with things staying the way there are.

To women's credit, they are more open than men to trying new things. They will eat at a different restaurant every week, go out of town to shop at a different store, and, in fact, women are more willing than men to explore things sexually in the bedroom. That's right, I said it! Women are more sexually adventurous than men. I believe the reason why men don't step outside the box sexually with their wives is because they either have the Madonna Whore Complex, which means they love their wives but they put them on a virtuous pedestal where nasty acts are forbidden, or men are afraid to pursue being sexually open with their partner because they don't want to awaken the sleeping tiger. It's easy to explore all kinds of hedonistic tricks with the other woman; she's probably not going to be around long anyway, but if they turn on that "Freak Switch" with the wife or girlfriend, they could create a monster that they can't control or turn off!

Unlike men, who typically slow down sexually when they reach their 40s, women are just getting started. And that's a huge problem with couples transitioning into their later years. Balancing the woman's increased sex drive with the man's declining one can be a challenge. It can also be very frustrating for the woman. That's why it's important to be open to explore other forms of pleasure to compensate for stamina. Longevity in a marriage is a worthy goal, but what good is a marriage that lasts 20 or more years if you can't have new experiences? To me that's not a healthy marriage; it's living a slow death.

Starting Over

Your partner shouldn't have to be your "everything"! You should continue to have your own interests and maintain your friendships with both men and women. If you had close friends before the relationship started, they should remain your friends, as long as they respect your partner.

We expect people to come into our lives and sweep us off our feet instead of expecting them to enhance the life we already have. It's about "Sharing our lives" ... not "Dismantling our lives."

You must "have a life" in order to have a life to share.

~ Michael Baisden

Losing Yourself
In A Relationship

Some people are so desperate to be in a relationship that once they click with a new partner, they immediately start altering their lives. Don't get me wrong; I understand that when you're in a committed relationship or marriage, your lifestyle changes. But there's a difference between making someone a priority and completely losing yourself and forgetting about your friends and family. That's not only unhealthy; it can be dangerous if you get involved with an abusive person.

Besides, wasn't your partner attracted to the person you were when they met you? So why change? And if you make too many alterations, you run the risk of your partner no longer finding you as intriguing. Sometimes people forget that even though they're married or in a long-term relationship, there should always be an element of mystery, something that challenges us to stay on our toes with our partners. Making yourself too available, giving up your hobbies and careers, and dumping your friends only puts the expectation on your partner to be your "everything"! That's a lot of pressure! Being up under each other 24/7 may seem fun and romantic at first, but after a while it can really get on your nerves. Next thing you know, one (or both) of you is looking to trade in for someone who is less needy!

■ ■ ■

While living in Miami, I met a woman named Cynthia. She was the inspiration for this chapter. Cynthia was beautiful, smart and ran a well-known marriage counseling practice. You would have never imagined from looking at her that she had self-esteem issues. But being physically attractive and having a nice bank account doesn't mean you love yourself. Some of the most beautiful and accomplished women I know are some of the most gullible ... and lonely. Cynthia was one of them.

Cynthia wrote: The night I met David, I was out at a restaurant having drinks with my girlfriend Susan. He was 35, tall, handsome, educated and great in bed. It had been years since I was in a relationship or had intercourse, so everything he did was blowing my mind. I was 49 and being turned out for the first time in my life. And it was that mind-blowing sex more than anything else that blinded me to the fact that I had completely transformed my life to make myself available to him 24/7. I'm sure my turning 50 soon also played a part. Although I was in great shape for my age, 50 is still 50 in a woman's mind; I don't care what she reads in the magazine about it being the new 30.

Susan tried to warn me about moving too fast, but like an old fool I got caught up and fell in love. It's kinda funny when I think back because I thought I was the one in control. I was older, I had a successful marriage counseling practice, and my social calendar was always full. But as my feelings for David grew, everything started to change. My "girls night out" with Susan went from three days a week, down to two, and then once a month. My entire world revolved around David — cooking his meals, running his errands, even playing stepmother to his two young kids. I had become a completely different person. To Susan's credit she never said anything negative about David, and why should she? I was the one who made the decision to give up my life for this man. David never asked me to do anything; he didn't have to. Since my children were gone and my parents were deceased, I had nothing but time on my hands. I was volunteering like the Red Cross. The only thing he was guilty of was taking advantage of me, but what man wouldn't?

I'll never forget the conversation I had with Susan a week before things between David and me took a turn for the worse. We were having dinner at one of our favorite spots at Bayside in downtown Miami. We sat outside with a view of the water and ordered appetizers and two glasses of Riesling. After a toast and a few sips, the subtle interrogation began. Susan was a dentist by trade, but she should have majored in psychology because she was a master at picking people apart, especially me.

"Thanks for making time for me, stranger," Susan said sarcastically. "I thought I was going to have to make an appointment just to see you."

"Ha ha, very funny! You know how busy things get around this time of year."

"Yeah, right," Susan replied as she took a sip of her drink. "How have you been, Cynthia? I haven't talked to you in weeks."

"David's great, I'm great ... everything is just great!"

"Whoa, slow down, girlfriend!" She reached across the table and gently placed her hand on top of mine. "I asked how *you* were doing."

"I told you. I'm fine."

"No, you told me David was fine. I asked about you."

"Girl, you're trippin'." I laughed uncomfortably and moved my hand away from hers.

Just then, the waiter sat the plate of calamari down on our table and took our dinner orders. Once he was done, I took a long sip of my drink and tried to stuff my face as fast as I could before Susan could ask another question. But she was a conversational Ninja. Before I could lift the fork up to my mouth, she got in a zinger.

"Why is it that every time I ask about how you're doing, you interject David?"

"David is a great guy, Susan. I don't know why you're attacking him!"

"I'm not attacking anybody, and besides, David is not the issue; this is about you!" She sat up in her chair and took a deep breath to compose herself. "Look, for the past six months I've kept my mouth shut and watched you go through this phase in your life, because that's exactly what it is — a phase. But you are too beautiful, too intelligent, too smart and too damned old to be rearranging your life just because you're having multiple orgasms."

"Excuse me!" I said, getting loud and defensive. "Do I tell you how to manage your marriage or your sex life?"

"As a matter of fact, you do, every chance you get. But for some reason people who are quick to give advice have a hard time taking their own."

"Susan, we've been friends since college, and I love you like a sister, but I'm not going to let you put David down just because I don't have time to hang out and gossip with you all day."

"Now you're the one who's trippin'. Remember, I'm the one who's been married for fourteen years, raising two kids, and I run my own dental practice, but you don't hear me making excuses for not having time for my friends." Her tone was serious. "You of all people should know the importance of having balance in your life!"

"But David gives me balance!"

"You see, that's exactly what I'm talking about. Everything is David, David, David! If I ask you if the sky was blue, do you have to check with David before you answer?"

I sprang up from the table, knocking over my glass of wine.

"Look, Susan, I'm 50 years old, driving a fancy car, living in a big empty house. My kids are gone, and I'm all alone. You have a life and a husband. I need somebody, too, dammit!" I stormed off towards the valet. "And you can stop calling me for these stupid dates!"

"The problem isn't your big empty house, or your fancy car, or your age; you're just dick-mo-tized," she screamed at me. "And don't think you're getting away without paying for your lobster; you owe me half on the bill!"

The weekend after my fight with Susan, I needed some "me time." I told David that I couldn't babysit his two kids while he went to play golf. He was livid. I guess he had grown so accustomed to having me at his beck and call that it never dawned on him to have a plan B. The following week I had tickets to a Miami Heat game, but he claimed he had a last-minute commitment, which I knew was a bunch of B.S. What man is going to pass on a Heat game unless he's getting laid? But the straw that broke the camel's back was two weeks later when he forgot my 50th birthday. Although I'm not big on gifts, you would think that lying in a man's bed four nights a week, cooking his meals and taking care of his children would at least earn you the consideration of a card, flowers, a call — something! But the only calls I got that day were from family and my best friend, Susan. I thought about not answering when I saw her number flashing on my phone, but she was still my girl and I missed her.

"Happy Birthday, Cyn!" she shouted.

"Thank you, Susan."

There was an uncomfortable pause.

"So what did you do for your birthday? Did you and David go out for dinner?"

There was another pause; this time it was much longer. I was so embarrassed.

"I haven't heard from David today! Now before you start dogging him out and telling me, I told you so —"

"Cynthia, hold on a second," she said, cutting me off. "I told you this has never been about David. As a matter of fact, I think he's a great guy! And I don't blame him for our fight, and I don't blame him for not calling you on your birthday."

"And why is that?"

"Because a person can only treat you the way you allow them to. And to be honest with you, if I was a man and a beautiful woman allowed me to play house with no strings attached, I would probably do the same thing he's doing."

"You're absolutely right. Maybe you should be my psychologist, not the other way around," I laughed.

"It's not about psychology; it's about learning to be happy with or without a man. And when the right one does come along, he won't expect you to give up your life to be with him. He'll want to share your life … not alter it."

"Okay, now I feel like I'm the one lying on the couch," I said, wiping the tears from my eyes. "How much do I owe you?"

"You can start by paying me back for that lobster dinner you stuck me with," she laughed. "Now get dressed, we're going out to celebrate the big 5-0. And I don't want to hear another word about men, kids or work. It's all about us tonight! Deal?"

"Deal!"

"I'll pick you up at 8. And don't forget your AARP card, we might get a discount on drinks!"

We burst out laughing.

■ ■ ■

Now you might be asking, what happened with David? But as Cynthia's girlfriend, Susan, stated over and over, this has nothing to do with him. It's about our choices. When she put his needs before her own, she was showing him that she valued him more than herself; that's not David's fault, it's hers.

For all we know, David was the perfect gentleman. Cynthia was never lied to, cheated on or abused. She made the decision to put more love and care into a man than into herself. I'm sure there are plenty of men and women out there who can relate to that.

But for Cynthia and millions of women who find themselves widowed, divorced or ending a long-term relationship, their willingness to settle almost always comes down to fear — the fear of rejection, the fear of starting over, and the fear of being alone.

The fear of being alone can be devastating if you don't learn to love your own company. Even people in relationships can feel alone with a person lying in bed next to them. Stop expecting someone to come into your life to make you happy; that's your job.

They should be there to enhance it, not to be the reason you're alive!

~ Michael Baisden

Fear Of Being Alone

I love being alone! I look forward to it, I plan for it, I celebrate it! I run red lights to get home so I can close my door and shut out the world to enjoy my aloneness. Maybe that's just the Cancerian in me. They say those that are born under the zodiac sign of Cancer are great at going into their shells for long periods of time. I know some of you may not believe in astrology, but it's true, at least for me. But for most people the idea of coming home to an empty house is terrifying. And the older they get, the more terrifying it is. The moment they arrive home, they rush to turn on the television, radio or get on the phone with friends and family to avoid hearing their own thoughts. If they have children, they stay engaged with them all day, leaving little or no time for themselves.

Some people are so afraid of being by themselves that they abuse drugs, alcohol and pornography just to numb their senses so they don't have to think about being alone. Others practically live on social network sites desperate to connect with other human beings. As a people person, I can relate to the need to feel the presence of other people. Each day on my Baisden Live page on Facebook and Twitter I post "Good Morning" and "Good Night" comments and attach beautiful photographs. I can literally feel the joy it brings to people who simply want to be acknowledged.

Unfortunately, many people don't have that connection, and for others it's simply not enough. Men and women both feel this void at different points in their lives and to varying degrees. Men don't talk about the fear of being alone, mostly because it's just not cool. No testosterone-filled man is going to call his buddy and say, "Hey, man, I've been feeling a little lonely lately; what should I do about it?" The chances of that happening are slim to none. Men live in a constant state of denial about being lonely. They won't even admit it to themselves. But the reality is men get just as lonely as women do; the difference is women will admit to it and talk about it with their friends, family or even a therapist, while men cover it up with multiple sex partners and countless female companions.

Men don't have the same need to find Mrs. Right. Most often all we need is Mrs. Right Now! Finding the ideal mate is not as important as having our needs met, be it sex, food, an arm piece for a special event, or day-to-day female companionship. A man's attitude is, "I'll cross that love bridge when I get to it!" Don't get me wrong; I'm not implying that men aren't looking for love or that special person to share their lives with, but men, unlike women, can be happy long term with one or more partners who are satisfying their sexual and social needs, especially if she's not causing drama and she's throwing down in the kitchen. Men will do anything to keep from feeling alone, even if it means having temporary women in and out of their lives for years.

The men who find themselves most lonely are the ones who have burned out from that bachelor lifestyle. They have been through enough women to know that it's about quality not quantity. Unfortunately, some of them don't wake up to this reality until it's too late. They wake up one day in their one-bedroom bachelor pad in their 50s and 60s with health and financial issues and a bad back. Now even they are no longer hot on the dating market. As they parade around in their fancy sports cars wearing way too much hair dye, they look silly. And they have spent so much money over the years chasing young women and paying child support, they are as much in need of financial support as women, if not more so. The nightmare for them is that they'll either end up paying a younger woman for companionship for the rest of their lives, or they'll meet the same fate as the women they have mocked: They'll end up alone.

I hope that men won't take offense at what I'm about to say, because I know it can be difficult for the average man when it comes to dating, but I wouldn't trade places with women for all the tea in China or all the gold in Fort Knox. The quality of men in our society is pitiful. Too many men are irresponsible, reckless and just plain immature. Men at least have the choice to settle down with a good woman when they're young, and even into their 40s and 50s they can find a relatively attractive woman who is holding down a decent job and wants to be in a committed relationship. Whereas, with men it seems like the older they get, the more they want to be single! It's a mature woman's worst nightmare. It's no wonder women are single and alone. I mean, seriously, fellas, would you want your daughter to marry someone like you or your buddies? If you answered yes, you're in the minority or you're delusional!

The result of this arrested development is more and more women find themselves doing the unthinkable — they are settling. Women who have spent their entire lives carrying themselves with class and dignity and even working out regularly to be a good catch, find themselves dating men who at one time couldn't get the time of day. But as women begin to see their options diminishing either because of their high standards, the lack of quality single men in their area, or the fear of growing old alone, suddenly their list of "must haves" begins to shrink. Suddenly, married men and men who are involved in committed relationships become appealing, even sexual exploration with other women.

No matter how much people boast about being happily single, nobody wants to grow old alone. But how far should men or women be willing to bend to avoid waking up to an empty bed for the rest of their lives? I posted this topic on my web page to get some feedback. Keep your paper and pens ready because these folks even took me to school.

Sharnell wrote: The fear of being alone is that fear of not having anyone to talk to when you just want to vent. Not having someone to hold you when you are scared. Not having that companion to go to the movies with. Not having the special shows that you watch together each week, somebody who just knows you without you having to say anything. It's that fear that when you are 45, 50, 60 you won't have that person to say, "Remember when we were that young?" or "Remember when we went to that place?"

I don't think it's a fear of being alone; it's more a fear of not having that person to remember life with. That one person who you can watch grow up, change, fulfill their dreams. Well, at least that's my fear.

Yvette wrote: I like your question; it had me in deep thought. I have spent many years alone. I must add I'm a young woman who enjoys my own company. Although I do enjoy social events, especially with family. But I must say what I don't like about being alone is not having a man's protection. Not having a man to stand up for me or defend me. And as I get older, I find myself retreating and avoiding certain things and situations. Please do not get me wrong; I'm not talking about fighting and all that type of silliness. When a man's presence is seen or felt. When other people on jobs, dealing with business, health, etc., know that this woman is loved by a man, that she has a man in her life, other men and people in general treat you (her) with a certain respect or it's less of a fight for the woman. Please understand I am a woman that can hold her own and I can stand my ground with the strongest of men, but why must I! Women may not want to admit it, but not having the protection of a man leaves a void!!!!!

Julie wrote: I was married for almost 26 years. I detest being single. I hate having to ask someone to go to events with me. Then I really hate going to events alone. My girlfriends tell me I don't know how to be a girlfriend and that I only know how to be a wife. I think they are probably right.

Aisha wrote: Women do face the "When are you gonna get married and have grandbabies?" question. It's a lot to take in and deal with and you feel like you have to find someone just to meet those "requirements." It doesn't allow you to find happiness, and sometimes you will choose the absolutely wrong individual to attempt accomplishing the goal. Time waster and now you have unnecessary baggage. Stay single, allow time to heal wounds, work on being a better person, most importantly learn to love and appreciate you. Get a pet if you're lonely.

Nia wrote: I will never get into a relationship out of loneliness again ... been there, done that; worst mistake I ever made ... sex toys are much easier.

Cheryl wrote: It's like this, not wanting to be alone I settled, thinking I saw potential, but it was nothing but talk. I call it the Keith Sweat, I'm Gonna Syndrome. In the end lack of responsibility made me re-evaluate the situation; after noticing that in two years there was no progression, I had to let go. I used to tell myself a man was not a need but a want, that I could take care of myself and just wanted a man that could handle his own. I now realize I deserve and need more. The next brother (after I take a long time for myself) will have to meet me at least halfway. Hell, he may even have to complete an application, which will go something like this: "Are you self-sufficient; do you have any pending or prior felonies, and do you indulge in recreational drugs?"

I will observe how he treats his mother or other female relatives and associates. In the meantime I will be preparing myself for my God-sent because in the end I too can use some therapeutic readjustments. What does it say about me when I keep picking these kinds of losers? I'm just saying.

Dionne wrote: Never again!! Sometimes we have to learn our worth as women and grow into womanhood. Some of us weren't taught to be happy alone, until the right man finds us. Speaking for myself, I saw my mother and other women in my family deal with certain behaviors that I find unacceptable. But as a child, you think what you see is normal. I think this is why many (good) women settle. We've been taught to just accept, allow and deal with almost anything just to say we have a man. Well, never again will I settle. To answer the question, I settled for and married a man to please people in my family that felt I was getting older, needed to have kids and be married. I was happy being alone at the time, but feeling the need to appease the older women in my family, who by the time they were my age, already had 3-4 children and had been married almost twenty years. I chose to stop this charade of a marriage this past April because I want true happiness with who God has made for me. I want that man to find me; until then I will learn to love being alone.

Iesha wrote: The effects of being afraid to be alone are you cheat yourself, waste a lot of years that you can't get back, miss a lot of men that could have been the one, and rob yourself of what you really deserved. What made me stop was looking at my children and not wanting them to follow in my footsteps, not to mention just plain old tired. If you can love being alone today, you'll have a chance at a better tomorrow.

Pat wrote: I have been single more than in relationships. I was in a 5-year relationship. I let that go and was celibate and doing me for two years. I enjoyed my time by myself and learned to love me and enjoy my own company. We as women need to take the time to love ourselves, and the right man will show up. We also need to start doing background checks on the men we meet, as most lie and are married or in a relationship. Love yourself enough not to share.

Louise B. wrote: I know someone who settled because she was afraid to be alone, and to this day she is still stuck. I often ask her, "How can you expect to meet Mr. Right if you keep letting Mr. Wrong block you?"

Leona wrote: Some women are looking for the perfect man; they have this long list of what he has to be, and like fools, they are sitting at home waiting for him to come knocking on their door. Well, it's not going to happen! Stop being afraid and get out there and meet people. Learn to love yourself enough and accept that you have issues which are keeping you single and lonely. There are times in life when you just have to settle for what's in your reach, what's on your level, and just stop waiting around for something you're not going to find. I'm not saying marry the first guy that asks you out or stay with someone who is abusing you, but doggone it, some women are lonely because they're too picky and too unrealistic!

Diane wrote: Being with someone (whom you've settled for) is like wearing cheap shoes that never get broken "in" but they just continue to hurt over and over! Cheap shoes may look nice on your feet, but they surely do not feel nice. I guess what I'm trying to say is, find a man who fits, and stop squeezing yourself into unhealthy relationships. You'll only ruin your feet (life).

Orlando wrote: I think for women, it's natural for them to feel more unwanted or alone when they feel that time is passing by and they have not fulfilled their natural gift of having kids or having a man. Every woman, in my opinion, should have someone that has her back. Yes, men too get lonely and fear being alone. It usually comes at an age when they feel they have exhausted all their options and age wears on them. No longer very attractive to the opposite sex lends to one thinking they will never be with anyone because he has treated so many as if they were not worthy of being loved the way she deserved it from him.

Lashan wrote: Women are afraid of being alone, not having companionship and not having anyone they feel loves them. Some women feel if they don't have a mate, they are less than a woman.

Phylesia wrote: I can't speak for other women, but for me it's not fear. I'm just tired of being alone. Since my divorce, I've completed a Master of Science in Applied Mathematics. I make a decent salary. I want to share it with someone worthy. I've been divorced for 16 years and haven't been in a committed relationship in 10 years. I'm tired of playing the role of both husband and wife, which is what it amounts to when you have to take care of everything to maintain a household. And in my opinion, I think there are more men who fear being alone than women.

Taiasha wrote: I personally don't think it's a fear of being alone ... more so the fear of being unwanted or undesirable. The alone part is not what drives the fear; it's the thought that no one will ever want you, the thought that you are not worthy of someone's love and affection ... and trust me you can still feel this way even if you are "with someone."

Kevin T. wrote: Michael, everybody fears being alone. Nobody was intended to be solitary. If solitary was not a personal hell, why is it used as a form of punishment in prisons? Men do fear being alone. I personally fear taking my last breath with no one there to tell me they love me back! I know a lot of men would never admit that, but it's true!

Ramona wrote: I'm not afraid of being alone. I am afraid of being without love. That love does not have to be romantic love, but it sure is nice to have a significant other that truly loves and cares for you. I think companionship is important. I do not think that you have to live under the same roof to have a secure sense of not being alone. There is much to be said for solitude and space. I think these two aspects are seriously underrated.

Art G. wrote: Hell yeah we fear being alone! It's bad enough having Saturday nights to ourselves ... imagine being 75 or 80! I'm looking for that chick now that I can be 83 with! I'll be that dude just sitting there on a porch while she talks her head off about something that only matters to her that I'm supposed to remember. I'll be more than happy to hold the yarn loop as she knits a microwave oven cover or whatever (shrugs). It's better than being alone is all I'm saying.

Finesha wrote: Both women and men are afraid of being alone. I think for women we hit a stage where we don't have a companion, the children begin to leave home, we don't have them to focus our total attention on, and if you're single by way of divorce, you begin to realize you've given away your best years. Grown kids when they leave home tend to not call. Especially when they begin to get married, have children, and jobs to hold down. This is the kicker for most men. The health begins to fail and here you are alone; you can't do as much as you were able to do when you were young. Friends are few. Family, too. Depending on how you have lived life, you don't have anyone to care for you when you're sick. You get tired of waking up alone and going to bed alone. I've found older men are just as desperate to have a mate as a woman.

I find the men in this stage are dangerous. They try and make a woman into what they want her to be, even when she doesn't have any interest in him. I think this is why the joke is on the old man who is vulnerable. Many of them lose their sexual abilities around 40, while women are at our peak at 40. My disappointment is that a lot of my female friends are going over to women. But I have seen the strongest of women put up with the most ridiculous relationship situations, all just not to be alone. It's hard to stand your ground. I find myself cutting my lawn instead of paying someone to do it. It's hard financially, sexually and emotionally to be alone. God just didn't make us to exist as one. He designed life so that we would become a family. That's why family is the basic foundation for communities. But I'm alone, and I'm going to stay that way before I settle the way my friends did. It's really pathetic!

Dolores wrote: I hear people talk a lot about being alone as if it only happens to single people. You can be lying in bed with someone and still be alone. You can be in a crowded room and still be alone. Being alone is a state of mind. I think both men and women fear it because of the unknown.

Everybody wants to feel wanted and needed by someone. It's only natural! We sometimes pretend that we're okay with being by ourselves, but in reality we all want someone to share our lives with, our victories with, as well as our pain and failures. We come in this world alone and we leave it alone, but it sure would be nice to share some of those great things that happen in between with someone you care about.

■ ■ ■

After reading those comments it made me wonder about a quote I posted some time ago. It read: "How can you be happily married if you don't learn to be happily single first?" Suddenly, I find myself conflicted with those words. Yes, we should all learn to enjoy our own company, but for how long? I agree with one of the comments that we are not designed to be alone. And no matter how much I love being alone, until I read those e-mails I had never entertained the idea that I might end up growing old alone. I spend so much time in deep thought, reading, writing and reaching out to other people that I rarely have time to myself to even consider the possibility.

But that's the importance of writing a book like this; it gives both the author and the reader a different perspective. Sure, there are people who need to do a better job of loving themselves, and learn to be their own best company and all that. But I'm beginning to believe that the real problem is that we don't openly acknowledge that we need each other in the first place. Women are busy proving they're strong and independent and don't need a man instead of admitting, "I am a damn good woman and I would love a worthy man to share my life with," emphasis on the word worthy. I think women have to be careful not to become too proud to admit they want, need and deserve someone to hold, love and grow old with.

And as for men, we must stop settling for these part-time "ego stokers" and "in the meantime" sex partners when our true desire is to have a woman we can love, cherish and provide for. Although men would never admit it, we are worse at being alone than women are. Our lack of maturity, lack of patience and lack of emotional security will be our undoing. Just like women, we shouldn't need a woman to validate us, and just like women we have baggage that requires some time out to deal with. Let's face it, we're all screwed up! But if we don't come to terms with our issues, we're all going to end up alone — alone without a partner, or alone even when we're in a relationship!

My advice to anyone who has been out of the dating game for years is to be patient, never settle, and buy a large bag of popcorn because the characters you'll meet on a date nowadays are more entertaining and scary than any movie!

~ Michael Baisden

Life After Divorce: Dating Nightmares

This was only supposed to be a short chapter, but after receiving so many responses on this topic, I could have written an entire book! In fact, those were the exact words of one of the women who responded to my question about how difficult is it for women to get back into the dating game after divorce. Now, fellas, I know we have our challenges. Some women can be a little high-strung, clingy and combative at times, but as I said in the previous chapter, I don't know any man who would trade places with what women have to endure on the dating scene today. According to the women I know and my fans, it's a real nightmare out there! Or as a woman so dramatically put it, "It's hellish!"

But let's begin by addressing the issue of restarting your life after divorce, and that begins with reclaiming your own space and time. This is a much easier adjustment than you may think since both men and women usually check out of the relationship mentally and emotionally long before the physical separation. When that day finally comes and your partner is gone or you leave with your last box, there is an overwhelming sense of freedom. It's almost as if you've been in prison and your sentence is over. I know that may sound dramatic to some people, but if you've ever been in a bad marriage or one that just wasn't working, you know exactly what I mean.

I do realize, however, that not every divorce is amicable, and many people go through a much longer recovery process than others. It's not always easy to adjust to living alone, making your own decisions, and getting to know new people after spending years getting in and out of bed with the same person. But at this point you have to chalk it up to experience and move on.

When I was divorced, I remember being excited about being on my own again. I had all these ideas about what I was going to do with my newfound freedom. I was with my wife for five years, so I can only imagine what it must be like to find yourself single again after 10, 15 or 20 years or more. When I blogged about it online, one woman described it as "walking into the Twilight Zone!" But the other comments were even more dramatic, especially when I asked women to describe how men and the dating scene had changed since they were single many years ago.

Gwendolyn wrote: I'm just getting back out there after being married 29 years. (Yes, I got married young.) It's been a lot of work. And guys are so different. And the game is just corny. Bring back the real brothers!!!!

Consuelo wrote: Men don't want to date anymore. They tell you their name and they are ready to have sex. If they see it's not going to happen, they move on to the next one. What happened to being friends first or just getting to know a person?

Tanya wrote: It's harder nowadays because women are too accessible, Internet, Facebook, etc. ... Men don't have to try with you because there is someone at the palm of his hands already waiting for him. But I'm a sucker for love, and I still have hopes that there is a great man out there for me. If I have to wait another 10 or 15 years, I'll wait for my Prince Charming. With the choices I've seen out here, it's not going to be that difficult.

Alison wrote: I guess because of the ratio being 10-1 women to men, guys are less likely to put in the effort or stay too long with one person if he's not getting exactly what he wants. And with technology moving faster than the speed of light, we've grown accustomed to everything moving fast, even relationships. But really, if you want something that lasts, it requires time. I guess I'm just old-fashioned. I swear I wish I could just get married again and be taken out of my misery. Being single is not what it used to be. Calgon, take me away!

Angela wrote: Michael, forget a chapter; you can write a whole book about it. I went out to a club with my single girlfriends, and the debauchery of today's singles scene made me rush home to my man and tell him if he doesn't marry me and I have to go back into that madness, I'll kill him. lol Women have it much worse than men, and it's our own fault because we let our standards plummet to the point where men don't even try to be gentlemen anymore.

■ ■ ■

Wow! Is this what it has come to? I thought it was bad but I didn't know it was THAT bad! Maybe this explains why so many women work so hard to maintain their relationships. It's obvious they're getting reports from the single women and the newly single women about the hellish dating scene that awaits them should they become single. But is this just the experience of young women? Surely older men are conducting themselves like mature adults, right?

Shelley wrote: I tried dating again, this time with a man in his 40s, but I'm not having any luck. I swear this man brought up sex three times in the first thirty minutes of our date. I wanted to check his driver's license to make sure he was 40 and not 14. Unbelievable! So sad this world has come to this.

Clarissa wrote: Michael, I thought at this age (55) the games would be over. But I was so wrong! I'm so confused by men that I haven't dealt with anyone in years. I tried to have a friendship with a man seven years older than me. He wanted me and his wife! I told him to take his old ass to the Swingers club because I'm not the one!

Marecca wrote: I'm finding that men even in their 40s and 50s want quality but do not deliver the same quality goods. I have two younger brothers and I love them to death, but I watch them place high expectations on the women they date but offer little to no return on invest-ment. When I say return on investment I mean more than just money. How about love, exclusivity, intimacy, patience, a kind word, being a friend and lover?

I told one of my friends, "I can't compete in this dat-ing world." As a woman you have to be as fine as Be-yonce, you have to cook like Rachael Ray, drive a 2011 or better vehicle, you have to be a molly maid, have a decent salary, and the list goes on and on before a man will even give you a first look. Now I see why so many women are turning to other women; it is complete mad-ness out here.

■ ■ ■

Marecca's comment is something I'm hearing more every day. The woman who carries herself with class and respect is at a disadvantage in a world where old and young ladies walk around with their asses hanging out and are willing to go to bed with a man at the drop of a dime — no courting, no dating, no nothing! They treat sex like a handshake. "Hi, my name is Lisa, let's get naked!" Even the more educated and well-to-do men are taking the low-hanging fruit. After all, why work hard for a quality woman when women are throwing their drawers at you just because you drive a Range Rover or Mercedes, and they're willing to be second, third or fourth in your rotation just to have a piece of a man? It's not that men don't want quality women, but let's face it, even highly educated and financially secure women are lowering their standards to the point where a man who is living at home with his mother barely has to lift a finger to get a woman's attention. As one man stated, "It's entirely too easy!" That was the perfect setup for the remaining comments I received.

> **Cynthia wrote:** If women weren't so accommodating, men would adjust their expectations! But where is the incentive? I've been divorced for three years now and still haven't dated. These women here in Atlanta will cut your throat for a man who is attractive and has a little money, or at least the appearance of money. And that's my issue. Why are we as women fighting over men, period? Our job is to make ourselves presentable and allow them to pursue us. At this rate in a few years men won't even know how to approach a real woman. But who can blame them? To be honest with you if I were a dude, I would be taking advantage of the numbers, too. It's so sad the direction our society is going in.

> **Jennifer F. wrote:** Mr. Baisden ... I'm 37 years old

and it is absolutely ridiculous ... the prior comments about guys getting your first name only and then wanting to have sex is absolutely correct. These men today don't want to date; they don't care whether or not you have interests, or even getting to know you as a person. The priority is to get you in the bed. And even when you trust them enough to have sex, they don't call back. I mean nothing, no calls, no texts, not even a freakin' e-mail. It really plays on your self-esteem. Please tell me, where are all the quality men because I'm a quality woman.

Denise C. wrote: When I got divorced and began dating again, I could have sworn I was teleported to an alternative universe where the men are the women and the women have become the guys. I'm sitting at the bar with my girlfriend in this popular nightclub in DC and I was amazed by how many women were sending drinks to guys. I guess I'm old-fashioned, but isn't that the man's role? And the women today are so aggressive.

The group of ladies sitting next to us would occasionally reach out and grab the hand of a guy who was walking by to get his attention. Every now and then they would pat a guy on the ass, and the guy wouldn't even flinch. Everything is all backwards. Men are no longer interested in the chase.

Ti Anna wrote: Men are so hung up on sex! I had a guy approach me the other day ... within the first minute of us talking, he commented on my breasts, lips and my legs and that he would be willing to climb the tree (me ... I'm 6 feet tall) ... all without even knowing my name! I'm so turned off by the lack of gentlemen in the world and why these "boys" feel it's ok to be so disrespectful and degrading to women!!!! Would they want someone speaking to their mama or sister that way?

Cynthia M. wrote: Michael, I literally had to fight a 52-year-old man off of me because after saying hello in the corridor three or four times, he thought it was okay to grab me and go for my butt. I was like WTH. My daughters explained to me that this is what is happening in the clubs and on the dating scene. Since that time he has been still trying to connect but no thank you. I told him, "Look, I don't know what you are used to but I am not the one." He said to me, "Oh, you are going to be a tough one." My reply to him was, "You are not used to standards," and he said, "You're right. Can I take you out to dinner?" Me ... blank stare and walked away.

■ ■ ■

After reading all these stories, it's hard to accept that this is the state of male-female relationships today. Now you see why reality TV is so huge; this stuff really happens. No matter what the age or profession of the men, the games continue, and regardless of the age of the women, the end of their frustrations is nowhere in sight. Every year thousands of divorced men and women re-enter the dating scene. Some are looking for new partners to marry and settle down with, while others vow "Never Again!"

Going through a divorce is never a good thing, but it helps to know you can go out every now and then to meet other mature adults. That's something you could count on 15 or 20 years ago. You may not be guaranteed to meet Mr. or Mrs. Right, but you could count on having a drink with well-dressed, well-mannered adults and hear some great music to dance to. Those were the days before they started playing hip-hop music at grown folks clubs. Men actually wore suits and ties back then. Everything is geared towards the younger crowd. And young crowds equal young minds. No self-respecting adult would be caught dead in these meat markets.

So where are all the grown folks now? We're either at special events, at our favorite restaurants with close friends or at home sitting at our computer surfing the Internet. That's life after divorce for most people, and it doesn't look like it's going to get better anytime soon!

Dating People With Children

If you meet someone who has children, you'd better be prepared to be a second priority, if not the third or fourth. Being a single parent is a full-time job with no days off. More than likely there'll be canceled dates, phone calls during dinner, and drama with the child's mother or father. If you can't handle that, keep it moving.

This is the reality of dating someone with children. I know because I have dated many women who had children. When you're young you don't really think about all the variables, probably because you're only focused on one thing, sex, and you have nothing to lose. But as you mature and your time and resources become more valuable to you, you realize that children can change the entire dynamic of a relationship. They can dictate how often you see your partner, for how long, how available they are to travel out of town, and here's the big one, how stressed out they are due to their constant arguments with their child or the child's other parent.

I have had entire dates ruined based on a single phone call. Either the other parent is playing games with the child support or changing their mind last minute about keeping the children. It's enough to make any sane person think twice about dating someone with children. The first order of business is finding out how many children they have and how many baby mothers or fathers are in the picture. These days it's not uncommon to meet someone who has children with three or more people. Be honest with yourself if that's past your limit; it's better to step off now than to be disappointed later after you were given the information. And the numbers can, and often do, matter.

Three or four kids with three of four kids' fathers or mothers can mean four times the headache, not to mention one big expense. I don't care how well-off that person is financially; unless he or she is rich, those children are going to become a financial responsibility. Going back-to-school shopping for one child is one thing, but three or four, now we're getting into some serious cash. But even when we set aside the money challenges, what about the drama that three or four mothers and fathers can bring? We all know the hell that one can take you through. Can you imagine the nightmare of having several people adding to the stress of your already hectic life? It would be unbearable! And with that many parents involved, there are bound to be issues.

David's story is the perfect example. He met a woman who had three children by three different men, but he chose to continue with the relationship. But the funny thing about dating a woman with three children, or even one, is it's all fun and games when the focus is only on having sex, but when reality sets in, it's time to man up or check out!

David's Story: Don't Bite Off More Than You Can Chew!

Trish was straight-up with me from day one. I had barely said hello before she announced she had three children. Later I discovered that in her previous relationship she had waited to tell the guy she was dating about her kids and when he found out, he bounced. So, she adopted this take it or leave it mentality, which I was perfectly okay with. Now I'm not going to lie; my goal wasn't to be in a serious relationship when I met her. But Trish was so beautiful I wouldn't have cared if she had ten kids, I just wanted to show her off and have sex. I think that's all most men are thinking about when they see a woman with an incredible body, and Trish was shaped like a bottle. I wanted her bad and she knew it. But I quickly found out that getting her into bed wasn't going to be that easy. She made me wait over three months before we became intimate, and she never introduced me to her children during that time; she rarely brought them up.

But not long after we had sex for the first time all that changed. She invited me to her older son's birthday party at a girlfriend's house. She told me that she was going to introduce me as a platonic friend and not to get touchy feely around the kids. At first I was offended, but not having children of my own I had to trust her judgment. It turned out to be the best idea ever. I had a chance to meet and hang out with her two boys, ages 10 and 8, and her daughter, who was 5. They were all great kids. The little girl was adorable, a real heartbreaker. I was so caught up that I didn't notice at the time that none of the fathers were there, which was odd for a child's birthday party, I later contemplated.

Fast forward three months. Trish and I had fallen hard for each other, and she was sleeping over at my place two nights a week. Up to that point she had never asked for a dime for herself or her kids. I went on a few outings with them but always as the "friend." She was very careful not to cross that line in front of her children. Everything I did financially, from buying clothes to computers, was completely voluntary, no pressure whatsoever. And it was me, not Trish, who brought up the issue of getting to know the kids better. On her way out the door after another incredible night of sex followed by an even better morning of sex, I gave her a passionate kiss and then grabbed her by the hand as she reached for the doorknob.

"So, when are we going to take this to the next level?"

"Trust me, David, let's just leave well enough alone. You know what they say, if it ain't broke, don't fix it." Right there is when I should have given her another kiss and let her out the door. In hindsight that was her way of saying, "I'm not ready, or you don't want to be involved any deeper, buddy." My reaction should have been like that robot on the TV show "Lost in Space" — "Warning, Will Robinson. Danger, danger!" But like an idiot, I took it as a challenge.

"I'm serious; let's start spending some time together with the kids. I can get to know them better and we can see more of each other."

"Look, David." She set her purse down and looked me straight in the eyes. Her expression was serious. "I don't play when it comes to my kids. Either you're all in or you're all out!"

"Of course, I'm in. You know how much I care about you."

"That sounds all good now, but I've been down this road once before, and not only did I get hurt, but so did my kids."

"I'm a 40-year-old grown man. I can handle this."

She paused, then put her arms around me and held me tight. "Please don't make me regret this."

"I got you, baby!"

"I'll see you at my place this Saturday at 7 for dinner. Don't be late."

The minute I closed the door behind her I knew I had crossed a line that I shouldn't have. Not because I didn't care for Trish, she was great, and her children were great, too. But that whole idea of getting closer wasn't coming from the real me; it was the sex talking. Rule number one in dealing in relationships, never make a promise or commitment within twenty-four hours of having great sex. I knew what I did was irresponsible and I had to do something about it. There was no way I was going any farther down that road. I pondered that dinner invitation for two more days. Going back and forth trying to convince myself it was "just dinner," but I knew better. This was my coming-out party, my "Guess who's coming to dinner" moment. Once I walked in that door there was no turning back. So I did what any responsible adult man would do. I invited her to come to my place and explained to her why I needed to cancel the dinner date, and I also ended our relationship.

Sometimes you have to come face to face with the reality of a situation before you start doing the math. I was 40 years old, single, a great job, nice home, no children. Taking on three kids was not the vision I had for my life. I wanted my own family. Trish was beautiful, classy, smart, doing well financially, but I did not want a ready-made family, and definitely not three kids. One, maybe; two, aaahhh, that might be doable under perfect circumstances. But three? No way, José.

As long as we were just having sex everything was great, but the minute the responsibility of those children became real, I had to get real with myself. Yes, Trish was upset, but she was willing to continue the relationship. But I knew being with her was not getting me any closer to having my own family. It's funny when I think back on it, being around her great kids made me realize that I was ready to be a father. Trish had her chance with three different men to start a family. I felt that I deserved at least one chance to have my own.

■ ■ ■

Sometimes the hardest thing to admit is that you don't want to date someone with kids. Hell, even people with children don't always want to date people with children. When you say it out loud, people think you're being mean and selfish. But I'd rather be called those things than to get involved in a child's life and then walk out leaving the child damaged. You have to be honest with yourself to know when a situation doesn't work for you. Or as David said, this "was not the vision I had for my life." I'm sure a lot of people can relate to his situation. Sometimes you have to be faced with a situation before you discover what is good for you and what isn't. I told you before that "Love Drug" is some powerful stuff. It can make you believe you can overcome anything, even be a parent to children you hardly know.

There are other instances where you can become so attached to your partner's children that you find yourself staying in the relationship for the sake of the child. I know because I've been there. Children do something to you. You can't help loving them. Which is why you should be extra careful about coming into their lives in the first place. If you don't intend on being there for the long haul, don't go down that path. I respect the way Trish handled David meeting her children. She waited three months, and then she made sure they were in an environment with other people. That's a lesson for parents to take away from his story. Establish an emotional distance between your kids and any new partners. Just because they are in their space doesn't mean they need to deal with the feelings associated with you being a couple. Let them get to know you as a person first.

■ ■ ■

Most people are perfectly fine dating people with children as long as they are well-mannered. But putting up with kids who are crybabies, disrespectful or throw tantrums is a definite hell to the naw! It's funny to me when I hear people say, "There's no such thing as a bad kid." Yeah, right. They obviously haven't seen some of these rowdy kids running around grocery stores and Chuck E. Cheese's. Sometimes you want to smack them upside the head along with their lazy parents. I know it's the parents' fault for not instilling discipline, but those are some bad-ass kids. I pulled some comments off my page related to the topic of dating someone with kids. My Facebook family didn't bite their tongue. They kept it real!

Grenetta wrote: I remember one date. I was seeing this guy who had a young child. That changed my whole opinion about dating someone with kids. He calls me up one day and says, "Hey, I'm in your neighborhood; can I stop by?" I'm like ok that will be great. He also let me know he had his son with him. I let him know that would be great! I love kids, and I also wanted to see how he interacted with his son. That is always a good indicator as to what kind of father a man is.

So he pulls up in the driveway and he and his kid get out of the car. I meet them, say hello, and invite them in. At that point everything seemed fine. After a while I notice the child getting playful like most young kids around 6 or 7 can get. So I suggest maybe he would like to go outside and play. "My son is older," I told him, "he can watch him in the backyard." He got all nervous and started telling me about the baby momma drama. I'm like dude he's only going to my backyard. OMG. But I told him I understood and I let it go. After a little more conversation, the child starts becoming more impatient and starts yelling and screaming. And then the crying starts, and this man starts trying to hold this kid down like a WWF wrestler. He had absolutely no self-control over his behavior.

Me being too old for this nonsense, I wanted to snatch this kid and say, "Enough is enough!" but I didn't want to interfere. That was his child, not mine. I'm thinking to myself, "You should be grown enough to teach your child how to act at other people's houses." I knew when my children went to other households, people would always tell me how well-mannered and respectful they were. Anyway, back to this clown. After an hour of this kid I had had enough. I suggested maybe he should take him home. I lied and said, "He looks tired and so do you."

After that date I never wanted to talk to him again. Don't get me wrong, I don't think I'm being mean when I say this, but your child's behavior around adults plays a major role in their thinking on dating a person with children. Your children's behavior is a reflection on what goes on in your household, and it was obvious his life was full of drama and mess!

Tonia wrote: At my age the first thing I need to know is how old are your children. I WILL NOT date anyone with babies. If your child is not old enough to date, I am not the one for the relationship. As we get older, we become more set in our ways. It is time for us to enjoy life not become mommy again pulling on my dress. No, sir ... not me!

Regina wrote: I'm 35, no kids and never married. It would be cool to meet someone just like me, but instead I've met a pretty amazing man who is divorced with two kids. Crazy thing is that what made my attraction grow towards him is how he takes care of his children. I met the kids when I met him. We've been just friends for five months but the friendship has blossomed to more. His situation isn't messy like other men I've met with kids. His ex-wife isn't crazy and she has her own life. They have both moved on. So far I think it's not so complicated dating this particular man with kids because of how cool everything is. He carves out time for just me, and I've kicked it with him and the kids as well. So far, so good. I guess my rule is, the kids aren't the problem. The man needs to be responsible enough not to have a messy situation where he's secretly having sex with the ex and not taking care of the kids. This creates craziness.

Yvette wrote: God, I know I'm guilty and ashamed to say I have dated some crazy men and brought them around my kids, even had them live in my house. My advice is if you date someone w/kids don't meet the kids anytime soon. Unless you're serious about the relationship, and I'm talking long term or marriage, there is no need to bring the children into the picture. I admit, I really messed up, and it's going to take some time for me as well as my children to heal. Please, parents, put your children first.

Diedra wrote: Unless we're talking marriage, it is not necessary to meet my children. I dated a guy for three years and he never met my children. I think women should stop jumping right into it with a man and her kids. It's nothing to play with. Too many children are hurt, abused or go through emotional turmoil behind their parents' bad relationships. I say marriage material relationships only, and you can't realistically know that for at least a year. And yes, I'm speaking from experience.

Antoinette wrote: If I decide to date a man with kids, I don't want to be a part of their time. I tell men up front, your children are your priority, do everything you have to do with them, for them and their mother, just don't bring them over to my house. lol And no, I'm not going to nobody's Chuck E Cheese. No kiddy parties, no amusement parks, nada. lol I would be good to your children, yes! I would include them in my gift list along with my children, but I'm not babysitting, not picking them up from school or activities, and I won't go with you to pick them up from their Momma's either so don't even ask!!

Corissa wrote: I have kids 19, 14 and 10. But I really don't care to date men with kids under 16. Why? Because most men do not know how to keep their child's mother in her place. They have no idea how to handle conflict appropriately. I can honestly say I do not have any conflict with my children's other half — none!

■ ■ ■

There are two important points about dating people with children that I want to make before we move on. The first is having an understanding that children cost money. If you are having sex with someone who is exclusive to you for any length of time, you can count on being one of the first to receive a phone call when something goes wrong. I don't care if you have met the kids or not. If you're being intimate with a man or woman on a consistent basis and they have children, those children will become your responsibility by default. It can be $50 here and there on a gas or light bill or a few hundred for new tires for the minivan. And don't be surprised if she loses her job, and your phone rings and she asks for a thousand or more for rent. To what degree she will need your support depends on her financial situation, but don't be so naïve to believe that you can enjoy all the perks without any liability. It's a package deal, Mr. Maintenance Man!

And ladies, that goes double for you since many women today earn more than men. If you are the breadwinner in your relationship, you can bet that if your man has children and he loses his job, you'll be the first to get that call for help with his car note or half on this month's child support. Don't laugh; it happens every day. You have to pay to play when kids are involved.

Lastly, and this is critical, make absolutely sure the person you're dating has a civil relationship with their child's mother or father. One of the biggest mistakes you'll ever make is getting involved with someone who is constantly fighting over child support, visitation, and, worst of all, the ex still hasn't accepted that the relationship is over. No matter what assurance you get from your partner, if the ex hasn't moved on, whatever issues they were having before you got together will only get worse. And God forbid you're more attractive or more successful, he or she will make your life a living hell.

Yes, children do matter when deciding whether to be in a relationship, but so does knowing if the person you're dating or about to marry has a crazy ex!

What About The Children?

The selfishness of some parents is beyond belief. They profess to love their child while waging all-out war with the other parent, usually for no other reason than he or she chose to leave for a chance at a better life. And even if the reason was less honorable, we owe it to our children to work it out for their benefit.

But revenge is an ugly thing. It cares about no one and it takes no prisoners. Meanwhile, our children are crushed by our angry words, tears running down their faces, and are left to wonder, "Why can't my parents just get along?"

~ Michael Baisden

Using Children
As Pawns

When couples split, the least they could do is act like adults, be civil and work together to raise their children. After all, the child didn't ask to be brought into this drama in the first place. Unfortunately, that doesn't usually happen. More often than not, one or both parents wage all-out war to make sure their partner will never be happy. And God forbid the partner who decided to leave finds someone new — that's when all hell will break loose!

But how do couples go from being madly in love to bitter enemies? Once upon a time, he was her protector and king and she was the love of his life, and they were going to be together forever. When they had their first child, it was the happiest day of their lives. They chose a name, took pictures and showed their child off to the world as proud parents. Their home was littered with photos of their son's basketball trophies and their daughter's awards from the spelling bee and dance recitals. And in the middle of the mantel was a large family portrait they took on their 10-year wedding anniversary.

But the divorce or separation put an abrupt end to that fantasy. One parent has left home with the children while the other packs up to begin his or her life as a bachelor. In the mind of the parent who never wanted the split to happen, the relationship is far from over. And if he or she thinks they're going to walk away and start a new life, they have another think coming. Somebody has to pay!

This storyline may have some variations depending on the situation, but the principle is always the same. Couples break up, the family unit is drastically changed, and somebody wants to get revenge! Suddenly, the children are put in the middle of a nasty separation or divorce and forced to choose between one parent or the other. But children who love both parents won't choose sides, which leaves them crushed in the middle of these out-of-control situations. In a perfect world the parents would agree on a fair amount of child support and reasonable visitation without expensive lawyers or the courts getting involved. But nine times out of ten that's not what happens, and it's not because couples *can't* work it out, it's because they *won't*!

Divorces today have nothing to do with amicably settling the affairs of the marriage; it's about getting even! If it were just two hard-headed adults battling it out over property and alimony, my attitude would be, "Be my guest, go ahead and make the lawyers rich!" But when children are involved, you have to step back, take a deep breath, and ask yourself, "Do I hate this person enough to destroy my child?" In their hearts the answer is no, but their ego and emotions are screaming, hell yeah, it's worth it! Forget him, forget her, and forget everything we own together, including the family. I'll burn that mother to the ground before I let him or her have it!

Of course, this kind of thinking is irrational, but whoever said separations had anything to do with exercising common sense, or any kind of sense for that matter. When it comes to divorce, you find out very quickly that common sense isn't so common. It's all about inflicting as much pain on the other person as possible. And the best way to do that is to use the tool that cuts the deepest and lasts the longest — that's right, the children.

It doesn't matter that the children are innocent; this is war, and in war everything is fair. Suddenly, little Billy is transformed from a freckle-faced 10-year-old with braces into a high-tech cruise missile, and brown-eyed Maria with the ponytail becomes an anti-tank land mine ready to blow the hell out of the other parent if he or she steps out of line. And even if there is no reason to explode, they will create one. All it takes is for the bitter parent to wake up on the wrong side of the bed and they are ready to blow some shit up! That's just how random these confrontations can be. It often has nothing to do with what the other parent has done, but as the old saying goes, "Misery loves company." And since they have the power of the children, why not pull the trigger whenever they feel like it and blow up everybody's peace of mind? *Boom!!!!*

Again, if it were just two adults acting like idiots, let them learn their lesson the hard way, but children shouldn't have their youth taken away or their lives ruined just because the parents can't get it together. No matter how bad the split was, no matter how much money is being sent or being withheld, children should not be dragged into the middle of the parents' mess. And shame on anyone who doesn't understand that!

When I interviewed William about his ex-wife using their son as a pawn, the frustration he was feeling was apparent and he didn't try to hide it. Even through this drama between him and his ex-wife started eight years ago, the pain felt brand new.

William's Story

My wife and I divorced when my son was 2 years old; he's 10 now. And every day since then has been one stressful situation after another. She's denied me my visitation on several occasions, refused to let him come with me on holidays that we mutually agreed on, and even after I took her to court, she would initially take him shopping and come back late just so I would wait two hours in front of her house.

I mean, at what point do women let go and move on? This wasn't even a case of me leaving her for another woman; I just didn't want to be with her! Never once did I miss a child support payment, and there were only four occasions in the last eight years that I missed my visitation weekend, and those were work related.

I sympathized with her for the first year or two because I understand how difficult it is for a woman to adjust to being alone again. But it's been eight years. How long does it take to learn to be happy with yourself, or at the very least stop making everyone else around you miserable?

I always hear women complaining about no-good men who don't spend time with their kids, but what about these crazy-ass women who fly off the handle for no reason and play games with their own children? That's not right. From my experience with talking to other men, that's just as big a problem as deadbeats, but you rarely hear this side of the story. It's always the woman who is the victim. But ask any man and he will tell you that he has at least two or three friends that are dealing with the same situation. My best friend has two kids, both girls, and he loves them with every fiber of his being. Those girls are his world. But it is that love that some women use to try to destroy a man. His ex-wife talks so negatively about him to his daughters that he has to spend the first hour of every visitation deprogramming them from her hateful comments. But he is determined to be there for those girls no matter what. But no man should have to work that hard to be a father to his kids.

Just last week my ex got upset over God knows what and told my son that I didn't love him as much as she does. Now why would you say that to a child? I was in another state at the time minding my own business, and she's verbally assaulting me over something that has nothing to do with me. Luckily, my son is smart. As he has gotten older, he is starting to see things for himself. I never have to say a word. He loves his mother but he can't wait to get out of that house. He talks about things like her negative energy and not being happy alone. It's amazing what kids pick up on.

One day we were riding in the car together and out of nowhere he said, "Dad, I'm never going to marry anyone like Mom." I was going to correct him but I thought to myself, "Why should I?" Over the years I had been sympathetic to her situation even to the point of defending her to my son. But he was old enough to know how he felt, and he had every right to express it. And to be frank with you, I didn't want him to marry anyone like her, either. So, I turned up the radio and kept on driving down the road.

I hope women understand that although they may be

giving the father a headache today, in the long term they are damaging their relationship with their children. I know my son will always love his mother, but I can guarantee you that once he gets older and moves away from home, he won't be spending much time with her, not unless she makes some serious changes. Not only is she ruining his attitude about her, but about all women. And women wonder where all these commitment-phobic and insensitive men come from. You're raising them!

■ ■ ■

After listening to William's story about how his ex treated him, a quote came to mind: "Hurt people, hurt people." His son's mother was in pain and he was her target. He may not have been her only target, but he was the easiest. She may not have had control over anything else in her life, but she controlled him. And like so many hurt women, she was abusing that control. For men who love being fathers there's nothing more painful than having your child used to beat you down; it's pure torture. It's also a form of emasculation when a woman toys with you financially and emotionally through your children. The courts give all of the power to the custodial mother. If the father wants to be treated fairly he'll have to pay for it with expensive lawyer and court fees. And that still doesn't buy him respect from his child's mother, regardless of how good a father he is.

During my 10 years on radio, I have interviewed men who were so traumatized they never wanted to have another child. You'd be surprised by the number of men who have gotten vasectomies just to avoid going through the trauma of dealing with another manipulating baby momma. I'll never forget what this guy said to me during one of my shows on child support. He said, "I got cut because I never wanted another woman to have that kind of power and control over me!" At the time I thought he was overreacting, but after listening to men over the years who have gone through this hell, I completely understand.

But men can play games, too! And they can be just as cruel as women. Once again the child is used to punish the other parent for not doing what the other parent wants them to do, the way they want it done. It's all about control. Stephanie has been through this kind of situation, but luckily for her, the man she had a child with finally grew up and started to step up to his responsibilities as a father. But that was after seven years of taking her through drama that would have put "The Maury Povich Show" to shame.

Stephanie's Story

Watching your child looking out of the window waiting for his father to drive up is one of the most painful experiences a mother could ever go through. I went through that for seven long years. And it is especially hurtful when it's a boy waiting on his dad. Initially, I blamed myself because I only knew his father eight months before I became pregnant, and he was married. But I told him I was not on the pill, and we both decided to be irresponsible so it was on the two of us, not just me. At first I didn't take him to court for child support, even though all of my girlfriends and family members were pressuring me to. "Girl, that man has a good job; you better go get paid!" one of my cousins would always say. I guess she thought I wanted to be like her, sitting at home with three kids by three different men collecting $4,000 a month in child support. But that wasn't the kind of woman I was. It wasn't about punishing my son's dad or getting paid; I just wanted help with the basics, you know, food, day care, medical, school supplies, and extra money to get a bigger place so he would have room to grow.

After my son was born, I insisted on a paternity test. I wasn't about to go through that nonsense of him denying being the father. Once the test came back, we agreed on $800 a month to cover all his expenses and that he would put my son on his medical. Well, I guess after he put my son in his medical with his other two kids, his wife found out; that was the beginning of the shenanigans. She made him take my son off his medical, which left me flipping the bill. But I didn't sweat it because I had decent insurance so I let that slide. Two months later, he started coming by the house after work to see his son, which I thought was a little odd considering that he had a wife and children to go home to. Usually he visited during the day on the weekend so this was a little odd.

Now keep in mind we hadn't had sex since I was five months pregnant. By then the romance was over and the stress of telling his wife took over. He was supposed to be the perfect husband now.

So after about a month or two of these late-night visits, he made a pass at me. I guess he figured I was healed up enough for him to have sex with me again. I stiff-armed him and told him it wasn't going to be that kind of party. He laughed and played it off like he was joking, but two weeks later he tried it again. This time I was not as polite and told him, "I made the mistake of sleeping with you once as a married man, I'm not making that mistake again." His response was classic: "But my wife and I are having problems. I don't think we're going to be together much longer." If you could have seen the expression on my face! I told him, "You must think I'm a damn fool!" And then I kicked him out and sent him home to his wife or to his other, other woman's house.

From that day through the next seven years, this man was never consistent on a payment, visitation or responding to phone calls. He told me straight up, "If you expect me to be a father to your son, I expect to have sex when I see you; otherwise, don't count on me being around." At first I thought he was kidding, but after two years of going back and forth with my son, it finally got through my thick skull: "This fool is serious!"

This drama continued for two more years before I took him to court for support. That only made matters worse. He told me he would never see my son again if I didn't stop the court order. I told him, "You can go to hell!" A few months later he was back with his divorce papers and looking to restart our relationship, but by then he had demonstrated such bad character I didn't want to be anywhere near him, so he went back to once a month visits, then once every two months, then once a year.

It wasn't until he turned 40 about a week before our son's birthday that he got his act together. I found out later his dad, that he hardly knew, had died, and he wanted to do better for his son. But it took seven long years, devastating pain and watching a child's heart get broken over and over again before he realized how much damage he was doing. All because I wouldn't lie down with him and have sex. Luckily my son was young enough to forgive him. Another year or two of this madness and we were both going to need to see a psychiatrist. But the sad part is that I have girlfriends still going through this same nonsense, and most of them are married. It's a shame to say it, but I'm one of the lucky ones. I only had to go through this mess for seven years; some of their kids are teenagers and haven't seen their dads in years. Can you imagine marrying some dude, and he refuses to see his own kids because the ex-wife refuses to have sex with him. Unbelievable!

■ ■ ■

What's really unbelievable is how common these stories are. People lie down and have children and then treat them as if they don't exist. Or they use them to get what they want or to control the other person. It's obvious we're not putting enough thought into whom we're dating and marrying in the first place. Clearly these people had issues long before we got with them. My advice to anyone who is thinking about having children is to pay close attention to the temperament of your partner. Ask yourself: Is your partner prone to being aggressive, argumentative or even violent? Does your partner take responsibility for their part when a problem arises, or is it always your fault? Does he or she apologize right away after an argument or does it take them days if not weeks to say "I'm sorry"?

And lastly, when you have issues within your relationship, does your partner resolve it between the two of you, or are they quick to drag outsiders into your business? These are all signs of a person you don't need to be involved with — period! Don't even think about having children with this kind of individual. Having children does not change the person you're dating or married to; it only amplifies their bad character. The insecure, immature, temperamental and argumentative person you're dating or married to will be the same one you have children with. So stop being shocked when you break up and they go ballistic; that's who they were all along.

Now that you know the signs of a potential separation night‐mare, the responsibility is yours to end the relationship, work out these issues before starting a family, or suffer the consequences! The choice is yours!

Deadbeats

My father was a deadbeat dad. I only recall seeing him three or four times during my childhood. I remember him coming by our home in Chicago and taking me and my brother and sister to McDonald's for hamburgers and hanging out for about an hour, and then he took off, not to be seen again for another two or three years. I remember thinking to myself, thanks for the hamburger and fries, bye! And I went back to playing with my friends. I was too busy practicing with my Bruce Lee karate sticks and watching *Battlestar Gallactica* to be concerned about his shenanigans. I never took him seriously as a father so there was never any real disappointment.

However, there are many men who do deal with feelings of abandonment by their fathers. I recently watched a program hosted by Iyanla Vanzant and Oprah on the topic of fatherless men. They were talking to a group of 200 men who were dealing with issues of not having their fathers around while growing up. I watched as men ranging in age from their early 20s to late 50s broke down in tears as they reflected on the day their fathers left home. In a strange way I guess I'm lucky. I never had the experience of having a father at home so I never had to deal with the pain of him walking out. I guess the old saying is true: "You can't miss what you never had."

People often ask me if I feel a void not growing up with a father. I would have to honestly say no. I grew up in the '60s and '70s when there were still plenty of responsible men and two-parent households in the community. There was a married couple who lived next door, three or four others down the street. A black married man owned the local grocery store. I saw my friends' dads be great fathers, and I had uncles who were married. So as far as I was concerned, I had the father thing covered. And, of course, I had James Evans from the TV show "Good Times." Now that man was the perfect role model for a father. We could use more examples like the James Evans character today!

It seems that every man who grows up without a live-in dad is labeled as damaged and bitter. For some reason it's taken for granted that men are better off with a father in the home. Well, I have a different perspective; I think that having a father in your life is only beneficial if he's a good father. If a man isn't committed to playing his role, the children are some-times better off without him. The wrong father can do more harm than good if he's revolving in and out of the child's life or setting a bad example. And let's not leave out the abusive daddies. Simply having a man "at home" does not qualify him as a good father. Real fathers engage their children, love their children, teach their children, provide for and protect their children. If a man is not checking those items off the list, then what good is he?

There is nothing more important to a child than having a man who is available and, most importantly, consistent. Yes, money is important. Yes, he should make his best effort to keep his promises. And yes, he should set a good example. But nothing, I repeat, nothing is more critical than being consistent with his visitation and contact with his children. In my opinion, blatant inconsistency is another form of child abuse. Bottom line! So fathers who have been out of their children's lives should either step up or step off! There can be no in-between, or as we like to say in Chicago, "No Half-Steppers!"

Which brings me to another issue related to deadbeats: How do you decide to allow the deadbeat back into your child's life after he or she has walked out? Is that the child's decision? And if so, at what age should they be allowed to make that decision? And what are the rules? I posed this question to my Facebook friends, and as always they were direct and to the point.

Isia wrote: In my situation and many others it will be the same as allowing a stranger into your kids' lives. If he's been gone for over 15 years with no contact by choice, how can you trust this person with your children? The fact that they share DNA may not be enough. I guess it will have to be their decision for me.

Terri wrote: Now that my two older kids are adults, it was their decision. They are aware their stepdad was the one who raised them, provided for them, but their biological dad always had access to them, and he chose to be absent. My children say that he is their friend because the time to father them has passed.

Melissa wrote: I don't think it should be the decision of the child. Children are vulnerable; therefore, it is the responsibility of the parent to do what's in the best interest of the child to prevent heartache from that other parent.

Jermaine wrote: Well I feel if either parent is trying to come back and be a part of that child's life, let them. It's so important to have both parents even if one has made some mistakes or as you said is a deadbeat. It's time to work together and be an integral part of our children's lives. I say this all the time; it's not always about the money because most kids don't remember how much money you had, but it's time they always remember. Ladies and men, no matter how angry you are, children need you both, so, yes, let them in for that child.

Levantria wrote: I allow my daughter's father in her life even though he is a financial deadbeat because the finances have nothing to do with their relationship; it has to do with him and me. It is important that she has healthy love for her father for her personal development. I love her more than the money so I never bring it up.

Jackie wrote: Two wrongs don't make a right! If the child is old enough, let it be their decision, but don't influence them negatively. Never talk or act in a negative manner against your child's other parent! It will teach your child forgiveness and simple respect for their parent. If you deny that relationship, you are in the wrong. Whether the other parent has changed or not is not a factor! He/she is also your child's parent! I got hurt emotionally many times from my absent father, but my mother never spoke ill of him and did not let us, either.

Wilma wrote: I say, give him three tries like in baseball, but after that third strike, you're out!

Tito wrote: No parent in their right mind should ever prevent the other parent from re-entering the child's life unless that parent poses some kind of threat or harm to the child's well-being. That's one of the major problems with co-parenting. A parent treating the child like they have sole ownership of a piece of property! It's not about them but should always be about what is in the best interest of the child, and in my opinion having both parents in the child's life is always in the best interest of the child! Now if the child is old enough to decide for themselves, then the parent should step back and allow the child and the other parent to work that out. A child needs both parents!!!!

Michelle wrote: It begins with forgiveness. You have to learn to forgive so that you can move forward without blocking your blessings, which in this case will also include growth for your child. It is not our duty as parents to decide if the absent parent is present in the child's life (exception to one's lifestyle that is harmful or dangerous). In that case some terms and boundaries may need to be implemented to protect the child. Both parents' common denominator must be the child's well-being in regards to physical and mental. We have to realize that as human beings we all make mistakes and that is a part of life. So in essence if someone makes the mistake of being an absent parent (and that may not always mean "absent from the home"), then somewhere down the line they decide they are ready to admit their mistake and face the reality, we as a man/woman of God must give room for just that.

■ ■ ■

I believe that deadbeat parents should always be given an

opportunity to make a genuine attempt at rebuilding their relationship with their child, emphasis on the word genuine. Some parents come back into their child's life to temporarily silence their own guilty conscience, and once they have dealt with their demons, they slowly pull away, leaving the child even more emotionally scarred and confused. Therefore, it is up to the custodial parent to vet the deadbeat to make sure their intentions are good and lay down rules and expectations. It must be crystal clear that the child's emotions are not to be played with!

It's a balancing act to protect your child while at the same time understanding the value of both parents being a part of their lives. The benefits can last a lifetime and impact future generations. I have seen firsthand the difference that a father can make in the life of a girl. My daughter is 22 years old, and I have been in her life since day one. Her mother and I had a bumpy start, but we both matured and worked together for the benefit of our child. When I lived in Chicago, I would see her on a weekly basis, picking her up from daycare and taking her to work with me on the trains. When I moved away to start my writing career, she earned plenty of frequent flyer miles traveling to visit me in the seven different cities I resided in. When she graduated from high school, I insisted that she attend college in Miami so we could spend more time together, and it paid off. Although she was busy with classes, work and her friends, we saw more of each other and developed a closer bond.

As a father I understand that I'm not just raising a daughter, I'm raising someone's future wife. She was raised to be independent and to choose men of good character, not just make a choice purely on emotions. One of the lessons I taught her was to pay close attention to how a man treats strangers; that's a sign of his true character. It's hard to know which lessons will stick, but so far she hasn't brought home a tattooed biker with spiked purple hair. Yes, fathers make a difference, even when we don't think we do.

As a young man I noticed a distinct difference in personalities and temperament of women who had effective fathers in their lives, the operative word being effective. By that I mean fathers who are teachers, not just disciplinarians. Fathers who are affectionate, funny, strong and good providers. When I was in high school, most of the young ladies I dated had effective fathers, and I dated some without dads, and there was a big difference!

The best example is my experience dating my high school sweetheart. One day I drove up in front of her home for our date and blew the horn for her to come out. Next thing I know, her father comes strolling out of the door walking towards me. When he got closer to the car, I rolled down my window thinking he was about to compliment me on how clean my ride was. Boy, was I ever wrong. He told me to step out of the car, and then he let me have it!

"Young man, don't you ever blow your horn when you come pick up my daughter, do you understand?" he said with a stern look on his face.

"Yes, sir!" I replied, wiping the stupid grin off my face.

"Be a gentleman and come to the door next time; otherwise, this will be your last date!"

"I'm sorry, sir, it won't happen again."

"You damn right it won't happen again!"

Man, he really put me in check. My girlfriend was in the doorway watching the whole thing. She looked sorry for me. After that incident her father and I never had any issues. We even shared a few beers over the next fours years I dated his daughter. But I promise you this, I never blew the horn outside another woman's house. And that's just a small example of the value of having an effective father in a girl's life. He taught her how a man should treat her, and he also taught me how to treat women, but my part of the lesson was secondary. It was all about setting the standard for his daughter.

Her parents were together for over 35 years before they divorced, but during that time she had the example of their marriage to learn how to play her role as a mother and wife. She was respectful, compromising, patient. She understood how to use the proper tone when we disagreed, and she gave me the opportunity as a young man to lead. People wrongfully think that the man's job is to step in and take charge, but the truth is the man's job is to choose a woman who will entrust him with that authority. That's one of the reasons relationships are in such conflict; we don't know our roles, and to compound the problem, we choose people who don't know their roles, either. It's the blind leading the blind.

I posted about this issue on my web page. I asked the question, "Do people with effective fathers make better partners and better parents?" From my experience, the answer is yes. But that's just my opinion. I wanted to hear what they had to say.

Tony wrote: Absolutely there is a difference. The women I have dated without fathers are much more hostile, combative, independent to a fault. They don't know how to let a man lead. They also tend to be very bossy, probably because they watched their mom struggle as a single parent. I don't mean to generalize, but in my experience women who didn't have effective fathers, as you call it, are not as good at being wives. I know there are a lot of factors that play into why they think and feel the way they do, but that's not my problem. I want a woman who knows how to play her role, not someone who is practicing.

Duana wrote: Generally, if a boy grows up seeing his dad treat his mom good and she's happy, it usually has a very positive outcome on his treatment towards women. Generally.

T.W. wrote: Yes, it does! It definitely shows up in her choice of men, especially if there's no real male figure to expose her to what good men do.

Lisa wrote: I believe any child, male or female, benefits from having a positive male figure in their lives.

The male figure shows the girl she is able to be unconditionally loved by the opposite sex; he teaches her who and what type of man she should be looking for later in life, and knowing her father loves her, she won't go looking for that kind of fatherly love elsewhere later in life. THAT being said, on the flip side I believe that too many people, male and female, blame too many of their problems and wrong choices on not having a father figure. You know right from wrong, and if you had at least one good positive parent or role model in your life, you know respect and unconditional love and right from wrong. Not having a father does not excuse you from your own choices. We all choose which paths to take.

Michelle wrote: Yes, there is a huge difference. My effective father taught/showed me that I was valuable. Also I know how a man is supposed to treat me and do his part to run a household. I so miss my father. R.I.P., Dad, you did one heck of a job raising a real woman. I just wish there were more real men like you.

Chase wrote: Some guys that never had a father will make the best fathers vowing to never let their child go through what they had to. It's all in the moral composition of the individual man.

Italia wrote: I agree ... it's an individual choice. For example, my ex had a wonderful father. His father was always doing something with the kids. But my ex didn't do anything like that for our kids. On the other hand, I know males where their father was absent in their childhood and they are wonderful examples in their child's life.

Dayatra wrote: Yes, having an effective father is very important. I had my grandfather, who was a great father, and my father was a very good father. Even being on drugs, he was still a good father; he had a great role to follow. What I can't understand on the flip side is if you didn't have a father, why you wouldn't want to give your child what you never had??? I'm just saying.

Victor wrote: Without a doubt it makes a difference! I had a relationship with a woman that had abandonment issues, and ultimately those issues tore us apart. Since her father was gone from the age of 5, there has been no positive male presence in her life. It ends up that music videos and popular culture are left to fill the void and determine what a real man is. A real dad treats his daughter like a princess and sets the standard for the men to follow in her life. Without that all-important presence, a woman could easily end up thinking that life should be like an episode of single ladies instead of what it really is — respect, commitment, loyalty and work.

■ ■ ■

When I think about my ideal partner, I envision her to be a woman who constantly speaks about the lessons she learned from her father and other men throughout her life. That for me shows value for a man's opinion and perspective. Women who grow up with fathers respect the role of a male authoritative figure but also accept his imperfections. Even good men make mistakes and let you down at times, but the difference between women who have effective fathers and those who don't is they don't hold it against them for the rest of their lives. They understand that their dad makes mistakes but he's still a good man. Letting go of disappointment is a part of moving forward in life. And those who have been abandoned by their fathers often have a more difficult time with trust and forgiveness. I'm not implying that fatherless women can't be good partners, because they can and often do. I'm merely making the case that the example of an effective father helps women have realistic expectations and gives them balance.

■ ■ ■

I want to close this chapter by echoing the point that was made by a woman in her post: Never talk badly about the other parent in the company of the child. All that does is destroy the child's self-esteem. Children often react by defending the deadbeat parent. Remember, he or she is a part of them, too.

Also, many custodial parents unfairly characterize the other parent as worse than they really are because of their anger and disappointment. The best thing to do is focus on your responsibilities and raise your child to understand that the other parent made a choice to not be in their lives, and leave it at that. In time children will make up their own minds about how they want to view the other parent. This approach leaves the door open for the deadbeat parent to come back into the child's life and do the right thing, or their actions will confirm that they are selfish and irresponsible. Either way, your conscience is clear!

When I look back on my experience growing up without a father, I can only recall my mother speaking badly about him once, and after that she left it alone. She went on with her life and provided my brother and sister and me with a safe place to grow. In the end it was my decision not to pursue a relationship with him. As I said earlier, I don't really think about him; he's a complete stranger to me. And maybe that's the most valuable lesson for the deadbeat mother and father to take away from their miserable failure. It's not that their sons and daughters will grow up angry and dysfunctional but that they won't remember them at all. It's a tragic outcome but, unfortunately, that's the world we live in. No memories are better than bad memories!

Maybe the answer to the problem is to educate the next generation about the importance of not having unplanned and unwanted children in the first place. Although there are plenty of children who are born into two-parent families, the majority of our children are being conceived in a situation where the child is not planned or wanted. Let's keep it real!

And the excuse for getting pregnant is always the same. The man says, "She told me she was on the pill." And the woman claims, "I took the pill but it didn't work" or "I thought I couldn't get pregnant!" Fellas, you can't have sex without protection and then get upset when the woman decides to have your baby. If you want to control your life, you must take control of your reproduction. And to the women thinking about trapping a man by having his baby, don't do it! All you'll end up doing is trapping yourself. Chances are he'll resent you, neglect the child, and this vicious cycle will continue.

Raise your hand if you have issues with that!

We sit in front of the television for hours, but we don't make time to read to our children before they go to sleep. We spend money on expensive cars and designer clothes, but we don't save for college tuition. We bend over backwards for the new man or woman in our lives, but we can't make time for a PTA meeting. Sometimes it really makes you wonder, do we give a damn about our children?

~ Michael Baisden

What About
The Children?

I won't cite statistics about how many of our young men are dropping out of school and going to prison; you already know the staggering numbers. I won't remind you about the increasing number of young girls who are involved in abusive relationships and suffer from low self-esteem. You're probably tired of hearing about it. Well, guess what, it's much worse than you think. The number of homeless families has risen dramatically since 2008 when the financial system crashed. Children are literally waking up in cardboard boxes or in the back seat of a car and heading off to school. Most people are in so much debt they will NEVER be able to pay off their bills, and many of them will NEVER earn enough to retire. What the hell happened to the American Dream?

Instead, we're all too busy watching the idiot box, getting our party on, and are so focused on sports you'd think we were co-owners of the team. Wake Up, People! While we're preoccupied with the latest drama on reality TV, our children are dying in the streets or dropping out of school at such a rate they won't be able to build enough prisons to hold them all. Which brings me to my next point. When did going to prison start being cool?

But change is never going to happen until those of us who have been fortunate and, in some cases, just plain old lucky stand up to help those who have given up hope. It drives me crazy to listen to well-to-do people talk down about poor people. It's like they developed a case of amnesia and forgot that once upon a time their asses were poor, too, or at least their mama was.

I have fought and marched for civil rights; stood up for the young men in Jena, La., the Scott Sisters, Trayvon Martin; and invested hundreds of thousands of dollars of my own money to promote mentoring and free health clinics for the poor. But I can't do it alone. All of us have to pitch in. All of us have to care. And all of us have to understand that our future is tied to our children. Most other cultures understand that. Not Americans, especially not black and brown Americans. That's right, I said it!

I used to have a recurring dream that I pull into a gas station and, while I'm pumping gas a young black man pulls a gun on me and asks for my money. As I look into his eyes, I recognize him. He was one of the young men at a mentoring program I met years earlier. But like so many men, I was too busy chasing women, making money or watching TV to be consistent. Now there I was looking down the barrel of a .38 special. The young man is so full of rage he's not satisfied with my wallet, so he pulls the trigger. *Bang!*

As I bend over in agonizing pain, bleeding profusely, tears begin to fall from my eyes. "I'm sorry," I say to him. He looks deep into my eyes as if he finally recognizes me, then he runs off.

The moral of this story is … we can pay now, or we can pay later. What we do or don't do will manifest itself in the lives of our children. Never be too busy to mold the future because we truly will reap what we sow.

■ ■ ■

Below are comments from coaches, teachers and mentors. I've been working with Big Brothers Big Sisters and the One Hundred Black Men organization since my One Million Mentors Tour; it was then that I learned the true value and impact of mentoring.

Motivator Joshua wrote: I mentor 20 teens every year; it really touches my life when I hear them say to me your prayers, your hard work and Motivation really helped me. You're like a big brother and dad to me. The young ladies always say they pray that their husband will have a heart and mind like mine and be a great mentor and father to them.

My response: Joshua, that's big, bro! I'm so proud of you. You helped change the direction of those children's lives. There's nothing bigger than that!

Tammy wrote: As a single parent a mentor helped me to encourage my son when he was in high school. Those conversations boys just will not have with their mothers had a strong positive impact on our lives. I am so proud of my son and was definitely grateful for his mentor.

Tiffany wrote: I have a 14-year-old "little" ... her eyes and brain soak up any and everything I say and show her ... I get to be a kid again, she reminds me to live and laugh. I think I get more from mentoring her than she gets from me. She is able to see a different life than what her mom is able to show her. I teach her to dream and dream bigger. Her self-esteem and motivation are growing; she is learning to focus, and having a positive attitude is half the battle to success.

Vanessa The Business Woman wrote: There was this little boy, maybe 10, and he was so disrespectful to everybody, adults included. One day he thought he was going to disrespect me. I told him that he wouldn't like it if somebody talked to his mom or sister like that, so don't do that. He continued coming by my house and started opening up. Then his sisters started coming to my house, opening up as well.

Come to find out they were raising themselves because their mom was too busy in the club or with guy after guy with no stability. I told them basically do not allow her to stop you from breaking the cycle. You go to school, have some respect for yourself, and get good grades. I told the boy they make jails just for our black boys so he needs to stop doing what he's doing.

Months later, I ran into them and one of the girls was graduating, and her family wanted to take a picture with me as they told her how I stayed on them and didn't judge them. Kids are our future, and it takes a village to raise these babies. Parents need to step up and stop stepping out once a guy comes into their life. I am a single parent, and I, too, was determined to break the cycle that was passed down to me. The kids in my neighborhood call me Madea. lol That's fine by me; if I can help that one child be saved, others can, too.

My response: Vanessa, that is an amazing story. If people aren't inspired to do more listening to that wonderful story, I don't know what will. If you died tomorrow, God forbid, your life already meant more than most. You not only take care of your own, but you paid it forward to children who were strangers. But you understand, as I do, these are all our children. God bless you, and may the universe give you back what you put into it. You are truly my hero!

Outside The Box

Everyone has a right to his or her opinion, but only if they respect the right of the person with an opposing one.

That's why I'm hesitant to discuss religion because nothing usually gets resolved except determining who can scream the loudest trying to prove their beliefs are right and the other person's are wrong!

~ Michael Baisden

Stop Playing With God

When I was hosting my radio program, "The Michael Baisden Show," I would hear rumors that I didn't believe in God. That's just ridiculous! For almost 20 years I've told the story about how my career began with me putting my faith in God and dropping to my knees in prayer with tears rolling down my face the day I quit my job. That wasn't an easy decision with a daughter to support and bills to pay, not to mention I was a college dropout with no job experience other than the military. But I put my faith in a higher power and trusted in my abilities that were God given.

I think people confuse my issues with organized religion with my relationship with my higher power. Those are mutually exclusive. Yes, I have issues with religion and some religious leaders, but my bigger issues are with those who sit silently in the congregation every Sunday while infidelity, molestation and thievery are going on in the pulpit. They are just as guilty as the perpetrators … now that's playing with God.

Every Christian, Muslim, Jew, etc., who hears "The Word" week after week, month after month, year after year and does not improve their life … is playing with God!

Every man or woman who auto-debits 10% of his or her income every month to tithe but never invests 10 minutes to help those who are less fortunate … is playing with God!

Every man or woman who is able and doesn't pay child support, and every parent who uses his or her children as pawns to get revenge … is playing with God!

Every parent who destroys their child's self-esteem and fails to protect them from molestation and abuse … is playing with God!

And every man and woman who stays home during an election after our forefathers fought and died for our right to vote … is playing with God!

You can't pick and choose which parts of the Bible, Koran or Torah to be obedient to and then chalk the rest up to "I'm not perfect" or "the flesh is weak." That sounds good for the first year or two, but when you have been attending services for 20, 30, 40 years and are still gossiping, cheating, cursing like a sailor and not improving your life in a way that is an example and inspiration to others ... you are playing with God.

I don't play with God because I fear God in a way that is measurable and real. I believe you reap what you sow. I believe in Yin and Yang. I believe that Karma is real. And I believe what goes around comes around! That's why I take care of my daughter and support my family. I donate my time and money to social causes. I'm one of the first to step up when there is a crisis in our community. And when I'm wrong, I say I'm sorry and I do my best to make it right.

Just because some people don't wear a religious label or walk into a building every Sunday doesn't mean they don't believe in — or serve — God. And that's another problem in our society; we are more concerned about labels and church affiliations than with a person's deeds or character. And that is playing with God!

Lastly, people often make reference to "The Universe" when referring to what the future may hold, while some think that is blasphemy. But didn't God create the Universe? Every element in our bodies originated from space. That's not blasphemy, that's science! In that sense we are all star children ... God's children!

It's amazing to me that the one word that is rarely used when referring to God is wisdom. Our society, especially the poor communities, has allowed our emotions to dictate our decision-making about everything from how we invest our money to our choices in partners and leaders. What we fail to do is tap into the most powerful gift that God gave us — our brains — and that to me is playing with God!

■ ■ ■

When I was growing up on the South Side of Chicago, I don't recall church attendance being the single most important factor in deciding whether someone was a good person or not. But today people want to know which church you belong to before they bother to ask your name. And since when did the ability to quote Scripture become more important than supporting your spouse or taking care of your kids?

A religious label is only respected when the person declaring it is living up to the principles of what that label represents. Otherwise, you're just another joker trying to con your way into someone's pockets or into their pants. And while no one is perfect, the bar to call oneself a Christian, Muslim, Jew, etc., appears to be getting lower every year. It is true that some of the most generous and successful people are members of organized religion; likewise, so are some of the biggest cheaters and abusers.

My point is there are good and bad people inside and outside of religion, and every belief system has its benefits and its issues. And when it comes to the big social issues, no denomination seems to have a better record than any other on the high rate of divorce, infidelity, unwed mothers, domestic violence, bigotry or deadbeat parents.

So the next time someone approaches you to join their institution, organization, group or clique, tell them to show you the statistics on how successful they are. If you want intelligent people to buy into your Christianity, Islamism, Buddhism, atheism, spirituality, etc., you'd better be able to demonstrate that it's working for you first.

There is nothing more irritating than hearing someone preaching about how great their belief system is while their own life is a mess!

Prayer Alone Is Not Enough

People are quick to quote Scripture, but somehow they always seem to manage to leave out the parts that require you to take personal responsibility. Going to church every Sunday, singing hymns and praying are all well and good, but is that enough? And that's my challenge to my church family; we have to make God an action word to impact more people's lives!

Too often churches are judged by how many people are in attendance and how much money they're raking in instead of the impact it has on the people and community. Many churches have become well-orchestrated productions to inspire, save souls and generate capital. And that's all good, but at the end of the day, what was accomplished? Has going to church become all about feeling good, showing off and being seen? Or is it about personal and social activism like it was back in the '60s? At the end of the day, it's not just about what lessons we get from sitting in church on Sunday, but whether or not we apply them.

My point is, if you're going to invest your valuable time and hard-earned money going someplace every week, you should demand to see results in every aspect of your life, not just watch as the preacher buys more expensive cars every year and moves into a bigger church. Who is that serving?

Millions of us file into churches, mosques and synagogues all across this country week after week, but the country is not becoming a better place, or a smarter place, or a healthier place. How is it that we are quick to quote Scripture but we can't channel that awesome power to stop making bad choices, or lose weight, or get back in school, or stop cheating on our spouse? The God and universe I submit to isn't just a presence, it's a force! And we're not tapping into it; instead we're using it as a crutch or a way to judge and exploit people. And everyone is to blame, the preachers, the institutions, you, me, all of us! Because deep down inside we know something isn't right and we're not doing anything about it!

Well, this is my attempt to do something! Change starts with an acceptance that change needs to happen, and then someone needs to start spreading the word. And I don't want people to think I'm attacking religion institutions because I'm not. What I am doing is challenging those who claim to have faith to start putting Scriptures and their faith into action. You can't pray for change but not vote; pray to lose weight but not eat less; pray to God to keep your lights on but pay your tithes before you pay your light bill! That's just not intelligent.

Too many of us don't balance faith and wisdom when it comes

to our relationships. That can be costly and dangerous. We believe that if we love a person enough and pray hard about it, there's nothing God can't do. But try telling that to the countless men and women who prayed for their partners to stop abusing them. Too many pray and stay instead of pray and pack, and they wind up dead. And what about the child who prays not to be molested again? He or she prays every day that their nightmare will stop, but the parent stands by and does nothing, or is too busy with his or her own life to pay attention that it's even happening.

Look, I understand the importance of faith; I may not be a religious man but I am a deeply spiritual one. And I know that having faith in someone, or something, is important. But what's also important is to understand that God has given us a power that helps us navigate, manage and discern the events that unfold in our lives. It's called the power of choice. But again, choice is an action word; maybe that explains why so many people choose to focus only on having faith because it's easier to just pray than to pray and do something.

The perfect example is a recent comment I posted on Facebook about people making better choices. The quote read:

Everything in your life is a reflection of a choice you made. If you want a different result then make better choices.

Most of the responses were in agreement with the quote; it's hard to imagine how anyone could see it any differently. But as always there are a few people who seem determined to take the easy way out of a problem.

Marlene wrote: Michael, we need to let God choose instead. If we put our decisions about whom we choose as partners and whom we lie down with in God's hands, we would make fewer mistakes.

My response: God gave us the power of choice and the intelligence to make better choices. We have to start tapping into the God within us and stop looking to the God outside of us to improve our lives. Use what God gave you like your instincts and common sense. I appreciate where your heart is on this matter, but we have to start taking responsibility for our choices and stop trying to put everything off on God. Let's start doing the hard work of learning ourselves, being honest about what we want, and setting standards and sticking by them. I think that's what God would want you to do.

Those who protest the loudest about sexual labels and open lifestyles are usually the ones most dissatisfied in their own sexual relationships or they secretly want to join in with the people they criticize.

~ Michael Baisden

I'm Not A Swinger, But...

For years the rumor has been floating around about me being a "Swinger." Well, I'm not and never have been. Yes, I know couples that "Swing." I've visited a club or two back in the day, and I produced a documentary titled *Love, Lust & Lies*, where I interviewed several individuals and couples. And I had a blast doing it! Swingers are some of the most down-to-earth, accomplished and secure people I've ever met. In that sexually charged environment they would have to be.

But here's my question: Why does it matter? If I were a swinger or gay or bisexual, would that take away from all the people I've helped, or the thousands of children my foundation helped match with mentors, or the fact that I'm a dedicated and loving father?

Just as with religious labels, we are hung up on sexual labels. But whether people are swingers, gay, lesbian, bi, straight or transgender, they all have children to raise, bills to pay and problems to overcome just like everyone else. The preoccupation seems to be with who's having sex with whom and what kinds of sex these groups of people are having. I mean, pretty much what all of this finger-pointing boils down to is sex. Maybe that's why America is the most sexually hung up country in the industrialized world.

When a politician has an affair in the U.S., it's front-page news, whereas in France and other countries it's an accepted practice. When young men here see a beautiful woman on the beach wearing a thong bikini, they hoot and holler like a bunch of jackasses, but in Brazil nearly every woman on the beach is wearing a thong; it's common. In the city of Amsterdam, the capital of The Netherlands, as well as 100 other countries, prostitution is legal. And just as a footnote, the majority of those countries have a lower rate of crime against women as well as a lower rate of sexually transmitted diseases. We think that by outlawing something or hiding it from sight that we can control people's desires. Just take one look at the war on abstinence and the fake war on drugs, and you be the judge. "Just say no!" doesn't work when it's a basic human desire.

And sex is the most basic of instincts.

Most human beings have a natural desire to have sex with more than one person in their lifetime, and that goes for women as well as men. Society tells us that you must choose between being single and abstinent or married and monogamous. That's it. But what if you want to stay single and have sex? Well, then you're labeled a shameful fornicator. And what if you want to have the commitment and security of marriage, but you want to have the option, with your partner's consent, to have sex with someone else? Well, then you're labeled a filthy adulterer and must be stoned to death. Okay, I'm just kidding. But I wanted to dramatize my point. The word for couples that engage in sex with other individuals or other couples is swingers. But that practice is also frowned upon, even though the majority of Americans are already in open relationships; they just don't know it. I'll come back to that later.

"Swingers" organizations are growing by the thousands. Each year more people are coming out about their open lifestyle and inspiring others to at least explore the option. Meanwhile, traditional marriage is dying a slow death. And it's not the fault of gay people or swingers. The truth is that everything from medicine to science and technology has evolved, yet our attitudes about sex, marriage and relationships have remained the same. And that can only spell one thing: D-O-O-M, or worse, B-O-R-I-N-G!

■ ■ ■

Did you know there are more than 19 major religions, divided into hundreds of groups, and over 30,000 separate Christian groups? I bet most people don't know that. And there are thousands of different food chains and restaurants, hundreds of different languages and dialects. There are options in cars and trucks, a choice between Facebook, Twitter and Instagram. And one of the most successful examples of choice on the planet is Pandora. Not only can you choose what music to listen to, you can customize those choices, by artist, by genre, or mix it up. Why can't we have those same options in our relationships? You'd think that was common sense, right? Well, if there's one thing I've learned in life it's that common sense isn't so common!

As I said earlier, when it comes to relationships the only "Church Approved" options are single, heterosexual, abstinent and married, heterosexual, monogamous; that's it! Even religious followers have the choice of hundreds of different options to choose from; meanwhile, the rest of us heathens and sinners are limited to only two. That's not only impractical, it's impossible. When are we going to stop living in denial about that reality? The majority of people reading this book are already in open relationships; they either don't know it or don't want to accept it. Most men and women step out on their partners at least once, and many are serial cheaters. That, my friend, is an open relationship. The only problem is only one of them knows it!

I wrote this chapter to encourage couples to communicate their desires, fantasies and preferences to save their relationships so we can stop this parade through the divorce courts. All we're doing is making the lawyers rich and destroying families, all because of the restrictive and unrealistic boundaries set by institutions with no regard for the uniqueness of the individuals in the relationship. To put it plainly, institutions don't have sex, institutions don't have to compromise in a marriage, and institutions aren't you!

But change is constant, even in relationships! I think most people, even those in monogamous relationships, don't characterize their relationships and marriages as "normal." If you're okay having sex with one person for the rest of your life, you still must customize that relationship to work for you. In my opinion, this historical decline in marriage is a direct result of people who are sick and tired of fitting into someone else's idea of what marriage should be. And the same is true of religion. More people are joining nondenominational churches because it serves their spiritual and social needs. They can customize the Bible's teachings to fit their lifestyle.

I realize that no matter how much sense this all makes, many people will not change their way of thinking. But just like with any outdated program, sooner or later you have to upgrade. The majority of Americans didn't want to let go of their eight-track tape players, either, but eventually they had to upgrade to a cassette player, then a CD player, then an iPod, and now it's all about Apps. People want the same options to upgrade their relationships ... they crave it ... they demand it! And if that upgrade works best for them, my motto is, live and let live! And if you're one of those couples whose traditional monogamous version 1.0 program works for you, then more power to you! But everyone deserves to have a choice!

If you're fortunate enough to find someone who loves you, understands you and accepts you, go for it! Don't allow the attitudes of friends and family to cause you to miss out on a good thing.

People who are happy want you to be happy regardless of the age or race of your partner. But those who are unhappy will always attempt to block your blessing. As the old saying goes, "Misery loves company."

~ Michael Baisden

True Love Is Color-Blind

Answer this question honestly: Do you think you would be dating someone within your race if race weren't an issue? Think about all the failures you've had throughout your life. Chances are they were with someone whose skin was the same color as yours. Now that's not an attack on your race; it's just simple math. We typically date within our own communities. But what if you lived in a community, city or country where diversity was the norm? Would the person of your race still be your first option? Be honest! The world we live in is no longer divided by black and white; neither should your options.

If you were serious about finding a compatible partner, you would be wise to expand your horizons. Mr. or Mrs. Right could be black, white, Asian, African, Latino, Native American, biracial, multiracial, etc. I would expect those in the church to be the first to say "Amen" since every religion that believes in a God must also believe we are all God's children, right? Yet church is the most segregated place on earth on Sunday morning.

Racism, bigotry and prejudice don't magically disappear when we walk through the doors of a church or other places of worship. We bring those same attitudes inside with us. Our children, fortunately, will not grow up in the same segregated world that we did, but we as adults still have a long way to go in being more open-minded about our intimate relationships. Some of us claim we're not attracted to other races, and in some cases that may be true, but more often than not, the reason why most people don't date outside of their race is because of fear ... the fear of what our friends, family and community will say.

Whether this is true or not I'll leave up to you to debate, but no matter what your attitudes are about interracial dating, if you're against it, you're fighting a losing battle. The fastest-growing segment of the population worldwide is multiracial children. But for now, we still have to live in the reality of the fear and ignorance of today's America and today's world.

There are still plenty of white, Asian and Latino women who have to think twice before bringing home a dark-skin man.

Professional white men, especially those in parts of the South, are still aware of how dating a woman of color could affect their chances for advancement in politics and corporate America. The only liberated segment of the population seems to be black and Latino men, because they are dating every race of women under the sun. They seem to be the least concerned about what people think!

But I do have issues with black and Latino men who put down black and Latino women in order to justify dating Asian, white and other races of women. There's no need to speak negatively about the women who raised and nurtured you just because you fell in love with someone of a different race. To me that's a sign of guilt or self-hatred, and that's not healthy. Love the person you're with because they are good to you, period!

However, we have to keep it real when it comes to black celebrities, especially if he owes his success to black women. Tiger Woods, Derek Jeter and other athletes who gained prominence and wealth through "non-black" sports don't feel quite the same pressure to "represent" with a black female partner. But could you imagine the reaction if Denzel Washington showed up courtside at a Lakers game all hugged up with a blonde-haired, blue-eyed white woman? Or if Tyler Perry showed up at the next *Madea* premiere holding hands with a beautiful, tall, tanned Latina model sporting a 20-carat rock on her finger? Black women would lose their minds! I hope I'm wrong and grossly over-exaggerating people's reaction, but I think if we're being honest, race still matters, especially when money and fame come into play.

It's a shame that in 2013 we're still not free to openly date and love whomever we choose. And the more public your career is, the more self-conscious you are. Having sex in private with someone of a different race is one thing, but parading them out onto the red carpet at the Grammys can be a career killer!

■ ■ ■

Earlier, I stated that women feel more pressure than men to stay within their race, at least from their families. But black women get pressure from everywhere, most of all from other black women, and oddly enough, from themselves. The black women I interviewed for my film *Do Women Know What They Want?* said they are either not attracted to white, Asian and Latino men or they feel a sense of loyalty to their race. But my question is, why are black women loyal to black men when the black men are not loyal to them? It's mind-boggling!

Black women, and women in general, must do a better job of supporting each other when it comes to dating interracially. Whether it's mothers, daughters, sisters or girlfriends, women should want to see each other happy, regardless of race. And here's a news flash for black women who are standing on the sidelines: white, Latino, European and Asian men love black women! And as the expression goes, "The darker the berry, the sweeter the juice!"

I know some of you are probably laughing while reading this thinking, "Michael Baisden is trying to start some mess!" My response is, people who limit their options for love are already in a messy situation. Life is too short to limit yourself to a certain race or age group. As you get older, you realize just how few people in this world are truly compatible with you. And if you factor in those who live in your city, are in your age group and are of the same race, the options really get slim. I always tell women, "Dating is a process of elimination, not inclusion! The more options you have, the more undesirables you can weed out until you find a good match."

Let me end this chapter with these sincere words of love and also instill in you a sense of urgency: Don't wake up one day and find yourself old and alone because you were too afraid, too close-minded and too loyal to your own race. You deserve to be happy! Have the courage to accept the love of someone who was brave enough to also step outside his or her comfort zone to love you. We can't claim to be all God's children on one hand and discriminate on the other. Life is just too short!

Commentaries

Don't Blame Facebook

Have you ever been busted cheating on social media? More than ever, divorce attorneys are using social networking sites to prove infidelity. Why a married person would be dumb enough to put e-mails, videos and photos online is beyond me. But the impact of Facebook is small compared to that of cell phones. Unfaithful partners can call, text, send explicit photos and videos, all from the privacy of their offices, cars and homes. You can literally sit across the dinner table from your partner while texting your lover.

So don't just blame Facebook; it's technology in general that is the culprit. All it takes is a laptop or cell phone, and you're anonymously plugged into the world of make-believe! Short, chubby men suddenly become 6-foot-tall record producers with six-packs, and out-of-shape women are transformed into former models and successful actresses. Married men claim to be eligible bachelors, and married women list their relationship status as "complicated" — code for "I'm married but available."

Blaming social networking sites for infidelity is about as dumb as blaming alcohol; they both only make it easier for people to do what they really want to do anyway. The solution to the problem is simple; start investing as much time into your relationship as you do in chatting on Facebook and texting on your cell phone! And to all you sloppy, stupid cheaters, I say, "Don't hate the technology, hate the player!"

You Attract
What You Are

If you want to attract healthy people into your world, start by getting rid of the negative thoughts, gossiping friends and dream-killing associates who are in your life now!

It might also be a good idea to stop having sex with married or emotionally unavailable men and women. And by the way, inappropriate phone calls, flirting and texting is cheating, too. Why would the universe deliver a good person into your life when your choices are so toxic? The law of attraction is real!

But if you're serious about attracting a significant partner, the best advice I can give you is to stop expecting to attract what you are not!

People kill me with their laundry list of what their ideal mate should be. They expect him or her to be intelligent, attractive, physically fit, financially stable, compassionate, honest, affectionate, patient, open-minded, drama-free and have a great personality. But what they neglect to ask themselves is, "Am I bringing the same qualities to the table that I'm asking for?"

Ultimately, what we end up attracting into our relationships is a reflection of who we are ... or the person we were too lazy or too undisciplined to become.

Food for thought!

Why Women Need Men Who Challenge Them

It's easy to become defensive when you hear the word "Challenge." Too often it's associated with going into battle or drama. But to be challenged also means to be stimulated intellectually or to invite someone to do better. Unfortunately, not many women meet men who challenge them in that way.

For the past 30 years women have been making huge strides financially and educationally. They read more than men, they graduate at a higher rate, they start more businesses, they travel more, and they purchase more homes. With so many advantages it makes you wonder, what do women need men for? The honest answer is, they don't!

I believe a man's true value is not in being needed. In today's society men should be more focused on being respected. But how can we as men demand respect when we aren't bringing anything unique to the table? Most mature women are financially stable; they have academic and book sense; and over 80% of them are holding down the household as single parents. Although a man's help would be appreciated, for many established women, money and help with the kids is not a "NEED"!

What mature and intelligent women long for is quality companionship and stimulating conversation with a real man who leads by example. As a young man I was told, "Nothing turns a woman on more than watching a man handle his business."

But just as a team is only as strong as its weakest link, a woman's development is arrested when she's not partnered with a man who offers the perspective of a strong man she respects.

My responsibility as a man is to bring my resources to the table — intellectual, financial, life experience — and challenge my partner to do the same. At some point, we will have a difference of opinion on a number of issues, but it is through those differences that we challenge one another to grow! As a man, it's not about being in charge or being right, it's about making my partner feel secure and challenging her to see the world through the eyes and mind of her man.

The challenge for us men is to gain more knowledge and

insight through reading, traveling and listening, to broaden our perspective so that an intelligent woman will respect our point of view enough to listen to what we have to say. We can't beat our chests and raise our voices believing this is the way to lead. We must lead by our example and strength of character. Only an insecure man would expect a woman to submit to his way of thinking when he hasn't accomplished anything with those thoughts. And only a woman who is a fool would follow a man who talks a good game but doesn't have anything to show for it. As I said earlier, most women don't need a man, but they definitely want a good one ... and a strong one.

To put it frankly, a woman can go to the sperm bank to make a baby or use a sex toy to give herself an orgasm, but they'll never create a device that can stimulate a woman's mind like engaging in a conversation with a man of depth and intelligence.

Stop Blaming
The Opposite Sex,
Maybe It's You!

Like many of you, I have good reason to be disappointed with the opposite sex. I've dealt with the liars, the deceivers and the materialists. And even when I've been honest about what I wanted and didn't want, we all know that people have a way of lying to themselves in order to be with you.

Then there's the group of men and women I call the "Irresponsibles." They mess up time and time again and refuse to adapt, grow up or take responsibility for their actions. It's always someone else's fault ... but not theirs.

And then you have the Fix-A-Dude or Fix-A-Chick! These are the people who have tons of potential but don't possess the discipline or work ethic to get to the next level. We've all gone into that Mother Teresa mode and tried to clean someone up, invest time and money into them, and in some cases married them or moved them into our homes hoping our overwhelming love and our example would spark a light bulb inside of them, and they would be magically transformed into the perfect half of a "Super Couple"! And as we all know, that never works out, right?

As you mature you realize that what you've been attracting into your life all these years was ... because of you. The irresponsible people you've dated was that part of you who didn't want to take responsibility for making better choices in a partner. Think about it. Why would a responsible person choose a person who is irresponsible unless they were subconsciously trying to avoid setting standards and principles and then standing by them? By definition a truly responsible person would never choose an irresponsible one. It's like oil and water.

Likewise, when you date the Fix-A-Dude or Fix-A-Chick, it's you who is broken and it's you who needs to be rescued from this ridiculous idea that dealing with broken people is a sign of good character. Well, it isn't. More than likely it's a sign of your insecurity. Some of us feel the need to deal with people who will not challenge us to be better. People with low expectations of themselves always seek those who are less enlightened, less accomplished and less confident. They need to surround themselves with people who will be overly impressed with them to cover up some internal feeling of inadequacy. Or let's go even deeper; maybe you feel that because you fix them up, they're more likely to stay. In other words, they will stay because they owe you something. But ask anyone who has been down this road, and they will tell you that the minute you fix the dude or fix the chick and he or she is back on their feet, they'll be gone faster than the last cold beer at a July barbecue!

Make this the year you start taking responsibility for your bad choices. You can't mature or grow by simply blaming others. No matter how much you complain about being lied to, cheated on, deceived or even abused, there's only one common denominator in each of these situations … it always happens to YOU! So YOU are both the problem and the solution. Now start focusing on the man or woman in the mirror and start working on YOU!

Starting today, I want you to acknowledge that allowing someone into your life is a privilege. You must be stingy with your space, guard your peace of mind like a precious gem, and constantly ask yourself, who deserves an investment of my valuable time?

~ Michael Baisden

The Value Of Time

Time is something you can't get back. Once it's spent, that's it! You can't buy it, you can't scheme your way into more of it, and you can't go back in time to change what you said or did. That's why you have to live life to the fullest with no regrets and make the best of each day, each minute and each second.

But unfortunately, we don't value our time. We take for granted that there'll be another tomorrow, another birthday, another lover. We think we have all the time in the world! I used to feel that way until I woke up one day and I was 30, then 40, and now knocking on 50. And if that wasn't enough of a wake-up call, my daughter just turned 22 and graduated college. Have you ever had one of those moments when you looked at yourself in the mirror or stared across the table at your children and thought, "How in the hell did I get here?"

I recently broke out my old photos; not on my iPad, but those old school albums with the clear plastic. Y'all remember those? As I turned the pages, I laughed as I reminisced on how cocky I used to be. I thought I was immortal, invincible, "The Man!" And then one day I woke up having aches and pains I never felt before. Don't get me wrong; I'm in the best shape of my life, but age has a way of creeping up on you and whispering in your ear: "Slow down, you old fool, you're not 20 anymore!" lol

I guess what I'm trying to say is nothing is more valuable than how you spend your time, emphasis on the word spend! Because that's what we do every day, we spend, invest or waste our time. To put it into perspective, consider this: Even if you are in the best of health, with the best genes, you can only expect to be on this planet for 70 or 80 years, and that's if you're lucky enough not to get run over by a bus or slip and bump your head in the shower. You just never know how much time you have left … right?

When you look at time from that perspective, you start to become more particular about who you spend your time with and what you invest your time doing. I don't know about you, but as I've grown older, I find myself waking up earlier. I want to take in as much of this thing called life as possible. I want to experience more of nature, have more adventures, see more sunrises and touch as many lives as possible before my time is all spent! I want the world to know I was here, that my life meant something … or at least have some damn good videos showing I had a great time!

So to you I say this: Don't waste your valuable time sitting in front of the TV watching others live out their dreams. Don't invest your valuable time in people who don't share your passions and your zest for life. And don't allow another day to go by without taking a moment to appreciate those who make life worth living, because you never know how much time you have left to enjoy them.

Conclusion

Having a plan is crucial; it gives you direction and keeps you focused on achieving a goal. But nothing is more important than finding your purpose. It's that job you would do for free; it wakes you up in the middle of the night with ideas; it's that thing you spring out of bed for and you can't wait to get to it. It's your passion!

Seek yours and you will find it! And once you do, pursue it with all your might!

~ Michael Baisden

Finding Your Purpose

Are you stuck in a job or situation you hate? If so, what's your plan to get out? As another year passes and we stare at our aging reflection in the mirror, too many of us find ourselves stuck in a bad situation. Not just because we're afraid of starting over but also because we don't have a clue as to how to get out!

Like many of you, I once worked at a job I hated! That's right, I said hated because I knew it wasn't where I wanted to be. And on a spiritual level the environment was not consistent with who I was or the person I wanted to be. For most of my 20s I was content with my job in the Air Force and then driving trains for the Chicago Transit Authority. But as time passed, I began to see my reflection in the mirror as I put on my uniform, and I would ask myself, "Is this it?"

And the more I had those thoughts, the more annoyed I became with my co-workers. I saw them as mindless robots living in the "Matrix." They didn't have a vision beyond picking up a paycheck and partying on the weekends. Then I became annoyed with my customers because I felt they didn't appreciate my hard work and dedication.

But that kind of resentment doesn't change anything, does it? All it does is make you bitter. My real issue was that I became angry with myself; angry because I was stuck in a dead-end job, angry because my life didn't have any purpose, angry because I didn't have a clue as to how to change my circumstances. And there's nothing that will drive you crazier than being stuck in a bad situation without a plan on how to get out!

For seven long years, five days a week, I rode those L trains back and forth from the West Side of Chicago to O'Hare Airport. While most of my co-workers were satisfied with their nice city paychecks, I found myself fantasizing about jumping onto one of those airplanes and never coming back. One incident that stands out in my mind happened on a bitterly cold winter day. I was working on the tracks with the maintenance crew flagging trains through the construction zone in 15-degree weather for nearly six hours. When my shift was over, I boarded the next oncoming train and closed the doors behind me. I was cold, my glasses immediately fogged up, and snot was running down my nose. I know I looked like a hot mess.

The train was crowded so I had to squeeze in between a family of four who had a ton of luggage and were all wearing large straw sombreros. I'll never forget how happy they looked, probably because they were escaping the bitterly cold Chicago winter. That was a defining moment for me because I wanted to be that family; I wanted to be on that plane leaving the cold weather; I wanted to be able to take my wife and daughter to a tropical place, and I wanted to do it without needing to ask "The Man" if I had enough seniority or vacation time.

From that day forward, my desire to leave became more intense. All I could think about was leaving that job. Each day it felt more like a prison. The perfect metaphor is the movie *The Shawshank Redemption*, and I was the Tim Robbins character who was determined to escape. All I needed was an instrument to help me dig my way out. That tool came in the form of a book. I don't recall which one I read first; all I know is that once I began reading, my mind completely caught fire and suddenly everything that was unattainable became attainable and the impossible became possible. I must have read three, sometimes four books a week. I was so engrossed I would get written up nearly every week for reading on the job, but I didn't care. I knew those books were my salvation, and nothing was going to stop me from taking in more knowledge. And it was that love of reading that evolved into my desire to write. As the universe would have it, that was the exact moment that Terry McMillan hit the scene with her book *Waiting to Exhale*. You may think that it is a coincidence or luck, but I call it an opportunity meeting preparation to lead you to your purpose.

I wrote my first book, *Never Satisfied*, in 1994 and began shopping it to literary agents and publishing companies. After the third rejection letter, I said to hell with it and published it myself. I received my first box of books on New Year's Eve 1994; by May 1995 I had quit my job to do what I know I was meant to do — inspire, motivate and lead. I ended up selling over 400,000 copies of the book, making it one of the most successful self-published books in history. As it turned out, those rejections were a blessing in disguise. We have to learn to trust where the universe, or God, is guiding us. The freedom to sell those books at a discount at events and out of the trunk of my car is the only reason I'm here today. You always hear the stories about rappers who sold drugs early in their lives. Well, let me tell you, I would have put them all to shame the way I was slinking those books. Having a hustler's mentality is exactly what it takes early on to get your business off the ground, and there was nobody on this planet that could out-hustle me! I was truly a man on a mission.

So do you have a plan that will lead you to your purpose? Because I can assure you that complaining won't solve anything. And to my Christian family, I say this with love … prayer alone is not a plan, either. If we spent as much time planning as we do praying and complaining, we would be closer to changing our situation. We must stop falling in and out of our comfort zone, take responsibility for our condition, and commit to making a plan … and follow through with it. As the saying goes, those who fail to plan, plan to fail.

But having a plan is just one step toward finding your purpose.

Once your plan evolves into your passion, or your dream, then you will be on the path for purpose to reveal itself. You may not even realize it, but from the moment you discover your true passion, you are already moving closer to your purpose. Suddenly, you will find yourself coming into contact with influential people who challenge you and present you with opportunities. Every relationship, whether intimate or professional, will reveal more to you about who you are, what you want and, most importantly, what you don't want.

My plan was to be a best-selling author, and as soon as I embraced that, I started meeting other authors and bookstore owners, and my then-wife began to find articles in magazines on self-publishing. That's how the universe/God works. It's the law of attraction, and it applies to everyone whether you believe in it or not! That plan to be an author turned into a passion to impact people through books, speaking, TV and radio, and that passion turned into my purpose of being a teacher, motivator and leader. Had I not had that initial plan, none of the amazing things in my life would have ever happened. And while I know that many others had the same plans to write books, the difference is that I was willing to take risks to turn my dream into a reality. I used my life savings to print more books; I quit my job and moved to Dallas, determined to make it by any means necessary. And that's what separates average success from greatness; you must have the courage to bet it all on yourself!

I meet people all the time who want me to invest in their business, and the first question I ask them is, "How much of your own money have you put into this?" The answer typically is a few hundred or a few thousand dollars. And then I ask them, "Would you bet everything you have?" Their answer is usually no! So I tell them, "When you're ready to bet everything you have, I'll think about investing." The lesson I am trying to convey is that I don't invest in businesses, I invest in dreams. And when a person has a dream, they will sacrifice everything they have to make it happen. Too often we are more concerned about money and fame instead of impacting lives. If there's one valuable lesson I've learned during my journey, it's that you will never reach your purpose with the goal of just being rich! You can be successful, but you'll never achieve greatness or find your true self. Every giant in business or the entertainment field tells the same story about wanting to change the world or impact people's lives. You must have a sense of servitude to be blessed with greatness.

The road to finding your purpose can be a long and frustrating one. What you think is your dream job is nothing but a dress rehearsal for the real thing. I watched Oprah Winfrey the other night talking about her life and career on her Master's Class program on The OWN Network. She talked about her journey from Mississippi to becoming one of the most powerful and influential women in the world. But Oprah didn't start out as the success we know today; neither did Tyler Perry or Bill Gates or Steve Jobs, all of whom have incredible life stories. And your story will be an inspiring one, too, because in order to reach a high level of success, we all have to climb our own ladders. Along the way we slip, we fall, and we have that moment where we don't think we can make it to the top. We have all had our moments of breaking down, sometimes in tears, wondering if we were ever going to make it through the next day. That's all a part of the struggle, the test and the molding to prepare you for greater things.

Oprah talked about how she got her first job at CBS radio as an announcer, and then about entering a contest where she was the first black woman to win, which eventually led to her becoming a news anchor in Nashville, and then to a local show in Baltimore. She knew reading the news was not what she wanted, but it was her pursuing her plan that eventually led her to her purpose. One day while getting her hair done for an event, she rushed into a salon that was not accustomed to doing black hair. The chemicals they used caused all of her hair to fall out. Desperate not to be stuck paying her salary, they moved Oprah to a new morning TV talk show, and the rest, as they say, is history. Her story had so many parallels to my own.

I hosted a TV show called "Talk or Walk" for Tribune Broadcasting in the fall of 2001. The producers had me in such a tight box I thought I was going to have a nervous breakdown! I wanted to be able to talk to my guests without being overly produced. I wanted to be myself. Oprah made the same comments about being stuck in front of a teleprompter reporting bad news every night. You can't force a people person and a teacher to be a reader. It just doesn't work.

I'll never forget while we were taping on the KTLA lot, during one of the many technical breaks I just started talking to the studio audience the way I do at my seminars. On this particular day, the break was unusually long so I wound up talking for about 30 minutes, nonstop. We were having a ball! When it was time to restart the show, a gentleman stood and said to me, "Why don't they just let you do what you're doing now?" I slapped myself on the forehead and replied, "That's what I've been trying to tell these idiots!" As it turned out that was one of the most valuable lessons of my journey towards my purpose; I found out what I didn't want!

Fear is another obstacle to finding your purpose. Too often we get comfortable with a little of something that is guaranteed instead of going for it all. I hosted a local radio show in Greensboro, N.C., on 97.1 WQMG on Sunday nights, called "Love, Lust and Lies." That was the beginning of my radio career, which led to my first full-time radio gig in New York on 98.7 KISS-FM on July 14, 2003. Many people don't know this, but I was No. 1 in New York without a paycheck. I hosted that show for free for nearly five months to prove to the station's general manager that I knew what the people wanted. Six months later, when I felt that I had challenged myself as much as I could locally, I told them I needed a syndicated deal to take my show national. When they refused, I threatened to quit, and they knew I was serious.

What they didn't realize was I never intended on being only a local jock, not even in the largest radio market in the country. I knew my message was meant for everybody, not just one city.

By January 31, 2005, "The Michael Baisden Show" launched nationally. I built that show from one station to over 80. Once again, opportunity meets preparation to lead to purpose. Just as Oprah did, I turned an opportunity in a small market and built it into a national superpower. And to this day no other radio personality with a music and talk format has achieved that level of success in afternoon drive. It was groundbreaking. But it only happened because I believed enough in myself, and in my vision, to have the courage to walk away. If you don't know your worth, then someone else will determine it for you.

■ ■ ■

Anyone who has achieved success will experience that moment when they ask themselves, how in the world did I get here? That moment for me happened on September 20, 2007, when I led the Jena 6 March in Jena, La. I along with Rev. Al Sharpton, the NAACP, the Urban League, church leaders and tens of thousands of protestors marched for justice for six black teenagers who were being charged with attempted murder over a schoolyard fight. Standing in front of that massive crowd made me realize that my purpose on radio was not just to provoke and entertain but also to lead!

That was the beginning of my metamorphosis from a radio personality who focused exclusively on relationships to an influential leader and a major voice to fight injustice. After the Jena 6 March, I put the influence of my 78 affiliates and 7 million listeners behind the election of then-Senator Barack Obama to President. I was proud that his staff gave me credit for being a major force behind his winning that election. The mainstream press may not have noticed, but anyone who listened to my radio program from the start of the primaries through Election Day knew "The Michael Baisden Show" was Obama central. And I was not shy about making that point crystal clear. Years later during the President's successful re-election, I took my mother to the White House to meet the President and First Lady. My mother was so excited she was shaking. Meanwhile, I was having another one of those "How did I get here?" moments.

From there I took on other causes, such as protesting the imprisonment of the Scott Sisters, supporting Free Health Clinics, and in 2009 speaking out on the death of Derrion Albert, a teenager who was beaten to death while walking home from school in my hometown of Chicago. I was so enraged that I felt compelled to do more than just talk about it. So I chartered a bus and traveled around the country to over 70 cities, donating $350,000 of my own money to encourage people to sign up to become mentors. I called it The One Million Mentors National Campaign To Save Our Kids Tour. The major mentoring groups credited my show for helping to sign up record numbers of mentors. Big Brothers Big Sisters even named an award after me, The Michael Baisden Inspiration Award. When they presented it to me at the Apollo Theatre in New York, again it was another one of those moments where I asked myself, "Is this really happening?"

And finally in February 2012, a year prior to my radio program ending, I sounded the alarm on the Trayvon Martin case. George Zimmerman, a self-appointed neighborhood watchman, followed Trayvon, who was visiting his father in Sanford, Fla. An altercation broke out and young Trayvon was gunned down. Zimmerman claimed it was self-defense, but nothing about his story convinced me, the Martin family or millions of others that this child was simply not killed in cold blood. I, Rev. Sharpton and other civic and community leaders led a march of over 30,000 people to Sanford to spotlight this horrible incident and to demand justice for Sybrina Fulton and Tracy Martin, Trayvon's parents.

Being there on that stage in front of thousands of passionate people and standing next to Martin Luther King III, Rev. Sharpton, Dick Gregory (renowned civil rights activist), Benjamin Jealous (president and CEO of the NAACP), Judge Mathis, Trayvon's family and many other national leaders, I felt at home. For the first time I allowed myself to embrace my role as a national leader. I knew that the crowd was there in large part because of my efforts in putting out the word. Unlike many radio personalities who only mentioned the case in a news segment, or only paid attention after the cable news shows made a big deal out of it, I completely shut down my show and focused on the case for four hours every day, five days a week, until the appropriate actions were taken. I was determined to get justice for that family. My attitude was, if this happened to my son I would want the same passion and attention.

As I was introduced at the rally and stepped up to the microphone to the cheers of the crowd, there was no ego-tripping;

315

I knew why I was there: for the family and for the people! From that moment my old thoughts of "How did I get here?" were gone. Because I knew how I got there; I earned it! My thoughts were more in line with, "Where do we go from here?" and "Where's the next fight?"

At some point you have to embrace your calling. And that was my moment! I had found my purpose! Now get out there and find yours!

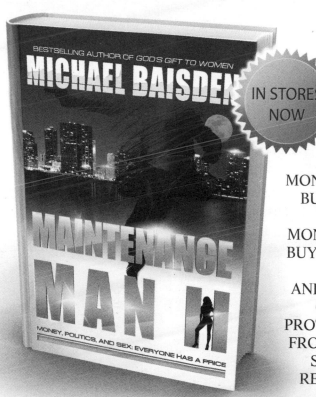

WOMEN HAVE NEEDS TOO

Malcolm woke up the next morning just before sunrise. He could see Alex through the window lying on the balcony naked smoking a joint. He grabbed his cell phone and poured a tall glass of wine and stepped out onto the balcony naked and joined her.

"I see you found my stash."

"It wasn't hard to find. You still keep it in the same place you did when we were at the music academy together," she replied while passing the joint to him.

"Old habits die hard?"

"Ain't that the truth?"

Alex took a long sip of wine and laid her head down in Malcolm's lap. They took turns taking pulls off the joint until it was gone then Malcolm thumped it over the balcony into the sand twenty stories below.

"This is what I missed most," he said while stroking her hair, "waking up to nothing but the sound of the ocean!"

"You know what I miss?"

"What's that?"

"I miss waking up happy," she said to him. "Ever since Derrick raped me in college, I've been searching for love in all the wrong places. I was always attracted to powerful men because I thought they would protect me, but instead they ended up trying to control me. And I put up with it all these years because I was afraid they would either hurt me or leave me, but I'm not afraid anymore" she went on. "I envy you Malcolm, you've always had the courage to do what you wanted to do. Me, I've spent my entire life trying to fit into other people's boxes."

"It doesn't work, does it?" Malcolm replied. He was thinking back on his relationship with Toni.

"No, it doesn't," she laughed sarcastically and took another sip of wine. "It's taken me all these years to finally figure it out: we should fall in love with our friends and just date the men we think we love. That way you don't waste time and no one gets hurt!"

Alex sat up and turned towards Malcolm. They were face to face. She set the wine glass down and kissed him.

"What was that for?"

"That was for all the years of being my knight in shining

armor, for forcing me to come on stage, and most of all, for last night," she said. "Thanks for making me feel beautiful and desired. Whatever you're charging for your services, it's worth ever dime!"

"Is that an endorsement?" he smiled.

"No, silly, it's a compliment." She took his hand and placed it on her breast. "How much would tonight have cost me if I were a customer?"

"Trust me, you couldn't afford me, especially not on your fiancée's salary," Malcolm laughed.

"Gary has a ton of money and it's definitely not coming from his government salary as a state senator. He drives a Bentley and a Porsche. I used to ask him where all the money was coming from but after listening to all the ridiculous explanations I just stopped asking and went along for the ride!"

"He's dirty just like the rest of them. There's so much money being passed under the table it's ridiculous. Some of them have the balls to pay for strip clubs and prostitution services on their government credit cards."

"Are you serious?"

"I have the receipts, photos, and videos to prove it!"

"Ooh, can I see?" she said jumping up and down like a little kid. "Please, Malcolm, please!"

"Hell no, woman, are you crazy," Malcolm laughed while trying to hold her down. "I *am* a professional. What happens with a Maintenance Man stays with a Maintenance Man."

"Is that your motto?"

"No, I just made it up, but come to think of it, it would look good on a bumper sticker."

"Do you have any video of Gary?"

"No, but there have been rumors!" Malcolm said. "All of these rich perverts have secrets and if any of them try to strong-arm me or my crew, I'll put on a show they'll never forget! All it takes is one click of a button and photos and videos of threesomes, bondage, and boy-on-boy sex will be all over the Internet!" he went on. "I've been in this game a long time, I know all their dirty little secrets."

"You make it sound so exciting!" Alex said while sitting on Malcolm's lap. "Can I be your assistant? It would be just like our music academy days. Remember how I used to set you up with my rich girlfriends back in school?"

"Ok, I think you've had enough to drink." Malcolm took the glass out of her hand. "This wine is starting to go to your head."

"Come on Malcolm! I'm bored to death! I know dozens of wives at the country club and they are just as lonely and horny as I am—and their husbands are loaded!"

Malcolm knew he needed new clients. His new crew was going to expect to start making money right away. Alex was just what he needed, someone with affluent contacts, someone he could trust, and someone who knew the drill.

"Okay, I'll let you help under one condition."

"And what's that?"

"Never use my name, never use the word sex and money in the same sentence, and never give them a phone number," Malcolm said with his finger in her face. "Just tell them about the escort service and I'll take it from there."

"Yes, sir," Alex said while guiding his finger into her mouth. "Looks like Bonnie and Clyde ride again!"

"Speaking of riding, your break time is over."

Malcolm lifted her up and carried her back into the hotel room then laid her down gently on the bed.

"There is one more condition I didn't mention!" he said while spreading her legs and then slowly licking her between her thighs.

"And what's that?"

"I want dinner… and dessert at least once a week."

She held him by the head and guided him down to her clit.

"Well, bon appetite!" she moaned and threw her head back. "Ahhhh!"

DIRTY POLITICS

MAINTENANCE MAN II

The sounds of fists being smashed against flesh echoed through the abandoned warehouse in downtown Miami. Vincent, who was wearing a ski mask, stopped beating the Cuban man who was handcuffed to a chair. He sat down calmly in front of him and lit a cigarette.

"Have one?" he jokingly asked.

The man lifted his bloodied head and nodded no.

"I don't blame you, these things will kill you!" he laughed.

He took a couple of long drags off the cigarette and then put it out on the man's forehead.

"Urrrgh!" he screamed out!

"That's for trying to register those fucking niggers and boat rowers to vote!"

Suddenly, the phone rang. Vincent looked down at the number; it was Senator Nelson.

"You mind if I take this?" he asked sarcastically.

He pressed the answer button and walked into an adjoining room, closed the door, and peeled off his mask.

"Yes, sir!"

"How's it going?"

"Everything is going like clockwork. Mr. Gomez and I were just discussing illegal immigration and conservative values."

"Well, I'm sure you'll make him see the light!" he laughed. "When you get done there's some business we need to handle over in Miami Gardens."

"What's the problem?"

"Some black preacher is getting his flock all fired up about voter suppression and civil rights."

"You want me to eliminate him or just scare him?"

"We don't need any martyrs this close to the election. Just send him a message—are we clear?"

"Crystal, sir."

"There's only a month before the special election. We've got to turn this blue district red in a hurry. The only way we can lose is if the black and Latino areas have a high voters' turnout. Now that we have a law requiring voters to show a state ID, that should reduce the votes by fifteen or twenty percent. And I've got friends who can knock a few thousand democrats out of the database, but that will not be enough if these voter registration drives continue to grow. My career, and yours, depends on a victory! The U.S. Senate today, the Presidency tomorrow!"

"Don't worry about it, Senator. I've got it all under control," Vincent said while pulling his nine millimeter pistol out of the holster.

"And don't forget, we have a meeting with the Kross brothers in D.C. next week, so let's make sure our poll numbers look good. In other words, get rid of all the trouble makers, starting with this goddamned preacher!"

"I'll be done here shortly and I'll be on my way."

"Do me a favor since you're coming back north, stop by Tom Jenkin's and pick up an order of barbecue."

"You want coleslaw with that?"

"No, just make sure you get plenty of hot sauce!"

"Hot sauce it is, sir!" he replied, then hung up.

Vincent walked back into the empty warehouse with his gun by his side and the trigger cocked. When the Cuban man saw he wasn't wearing his mask, he panicked, pulling and jerking on the handcuffs as hard he could, trying to break loose of the metal chair.

"Looks like play time is over!" Vincent said without emotion while staring at his watch. "Tick tock, tick tock!"

"No, please no!" he screamed. "I have a wife and kids!"

"You should've thought about that when I warned you the first time," Vincent said, pointing the gun at the man's head. "You people just don't get it, do you? Democracy is an illusion; those who have the money have the power!" Then he pulled the trigger.

About Michael Baisden

Michael Baisden is undeniably one of the most influential and engaging personalities in radio history. His meteoric rise to #1 redefined radio with the numbers to back it up. Heard in over 100 citics nationwide, the show had 7 million loyal listeners daily. Baisden recently stepped down after 10 years.

As a college dropout, former Air Force Sergeant, single parent and transit workcr from the South Side of Chicago, he wanted his life to mean something. That opportunity came when he stepped out on faith to live his dream of becoming a writer. That courageous step resulted in 5 best selling books with nearly 2 million in print, 2 of his titles being adapted into stage plays playing to sold out crowds across the United States and 2 national television shows.

Baisden is a noted speaker, television talk show host, film producer, social activist, philanthropist, and has been presented with numerous awards. He was honored by Big Brothers Big Sisters with the Michael Baisden Inspiration Award. The award named in his honor will be given in future years to people who are dedicating themselves to actively recruiting mentors.

Michael believes that "books change lives" and he is living proof! Stay tuned and his next chapter and his legacy continues...

Find Michael on Facebook: BaisdenLive
Follow Michael on Twitter: @ BaisdenLive
View Michael on YouTube: /BaisdenLive

www.MichaelBaisden.com
www.BaisdenLive.com
www.MingleCity.com

www.RaiseYourHandIfYouHaveIssues.com

THE MICHAEL BAISDEN SHOW
Informative, Engaging...Funny!

As one of the most influential personalities in the country, Michael
has hosted sold out relationships
seminars for over 20 years and broadcasted to over 7 million
listeners in over 100 cities nationwide as host of The Michael
Baisden Radio Show. Recently, Michael stepped down from his
radio program after 10 years to focus his attention on mentoring
and public speaking. For more information and to listen to
rewinds from the popular show, go to: **www.BaisdenLive.com**

SOCIAL NETWORKING:

www.MingleCity.com is the online
community for drama-free adults. It
is a place for singles, couples, groups
and friends to interact with other
like-minded members in their area, across the country and the
world. Create your own personal webpage, invite your friends,
start or join groups, find events, chat, blog, post your favorite
photos and videos.

SOCIAL MEDIA @ BAISDENLIVE:

Follow Michael @ Twitter: **Like Michael on Facebook @**
BAISDENLIVE   **BAISDENLIVE**

Tune In on YouTube @
BAISDENLIVE

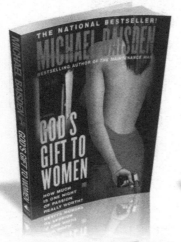

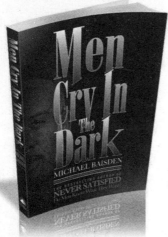
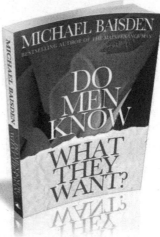

DO MEN KNOW WHAT THEY WANT?

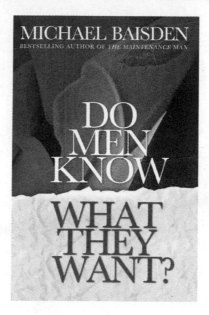

I wrote this book because I was sick and tired of scientific theories about why men do what they do. *Never Satisfied* is a collection of interviews about how men feel about sex, relationships, and monogamy. Do men know what they want, and more importantly, will women listen?

Men expect woman to have it all, nice figure, sense of humor, master chef, and sex guru. But she must be careful not to be too whorish otherwise he will suspect her of foul play. "Where did you learn that trick?"

Insecure men are intimidated by sexually confident women!
~ *Michael Baisden*

THE MAINTENANCE MAN I
COLLECTOR'S EDITION

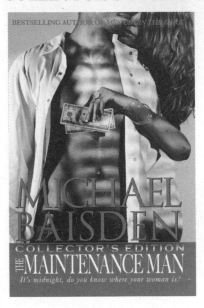

Every Woman's Dream: Malcolm Tremell is handsome, charismatic and a great lover; but in his world sex is not a game...it's serious business.

Every week his schedule is booked with secret rendezvous, extravagant dinners and sessions of passionate love making, all for the right price.

But Malcolm begins to reflect on his gigolo lifestyle when he meets Toni, a talented dancer and choreographer.

Would her love would transform him into the man he wants to be and the man she needs to make both their lives complete?

GOD'S GIFT TO WOMEN

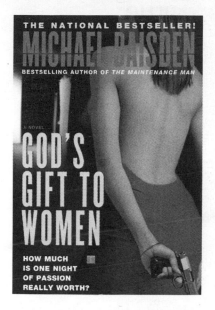

A smooth talker. An even better listener. And handsome as heaven on earth. He is God's Gift to Women.

Julian Payne gets into bed with millions of women every night. As an after-hours radio talk-show host, Julian captivates his female audience with his deep voice and sensitive spirit. Women can't get enough: They call in, begging for his advice about love, lust, commitment, and betrayal. Julian provides his listeners with the blunt male perspective, and he always has the right thing to say. But when it comes to his own romantic life, or lack thereof, he's at a loss for words.

A widower and father to ten-year-old Samantha, Julian wants nothing more than to settle down again with the right woman. Just when he thinks he's found her in Dr. Terri Ross — smart, stunning, and with her own counseling practice -- Julian is confronted by a ghost from the past: Olivia Brown, a woman with whom he had a one-night stand. Suddenly Julian finds himself in a situation with a woman who's determined to win him over... or make his life a living hell.

Michael Baisden's hottest offering yet, *God's Gift to Women* is a compelling tale about the consequences of sex with a stranger.

MEN CRY IN THE DARK

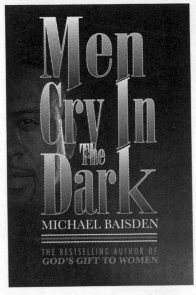

Men Cry In The Dark is an entertaining and realistic novel about fatherhood, interracial dating, and the fear of love and commitment from a man's perspective. Michael Baisden has courageously defied the stereotypes to prove once and for all that men love their children, cherish their women, and yes, even cry.

Michael Baisden is a Nationally Syndicated Radio Personality, TV Show Host, and Social Activist. He has dedicated his career to supporting mentoring programs and stirring up heated debate, both with equal passion.

"The truth will always be controversial; I just prefer not to hide from it!"

~ *Michael Baisden*

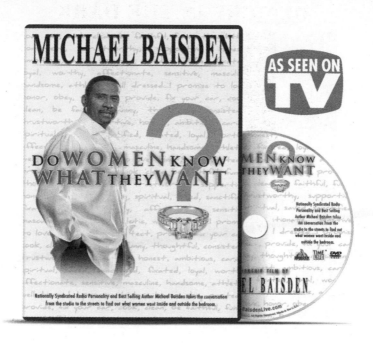

DO WOMEN KNOW WHAT THEY WANT?

What started out as a cordial conversation with one simple question "Do Women Know What They Want?" exploded into a battle of the sexes that will have you laughing hysterically one minute and shouting at the screen the next!

No longer anonymous voices on the radio, can men be honest about their multiple relationships, interracial dating, and why they choose to date but not marry some women? And can women admit to having afairs with married men, take responsibility for their bad choices, and explain why they fake it?

Suggested Retail Price: $16.95
Available in Cut and a *Too Hot for TV,* UN-CUT version!

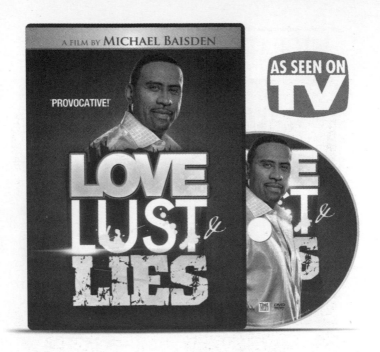

LOVE, LUST & LIES

We've all seen documentaries that deal with relationships and sexuality, such as "Real Sex" on HBO. But if you're like me, you've thought about how exciting it would be to experience a program that deals with these issues from the perspective of people of color. Well the wait is over.

"It's amazing to me how many people are afraid to be open about what they want inside and outside the bedroom," Michael says. "Hopefully, after watching these interviews they'll be more willing to explore their sexuality and to discuss issues such as infidelity, adult toys, and the swinging lifestyle."

Suggested Retail Price: $16.95

Available in Cut and a *Too Hot for TV*, UN-CUT version!

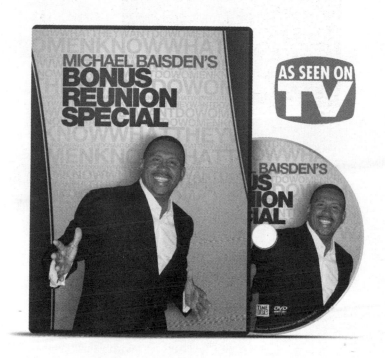

MICHAEL BAISDEN'S
BONUS REUNION SPECIAL

Filmmaker Michael Baisden digs even deeper into what women really want in this special reunion DVD. He unites some of the most outspoken men and women interviewed from across the country for one hot night of up close and personal Q&A!

Only Available Online
Suggested Retail Price: $16.95

Congratulations
Michael Baisden
The *MOST* Influential Man In Radio

THE *Michael Baisden* SHOW